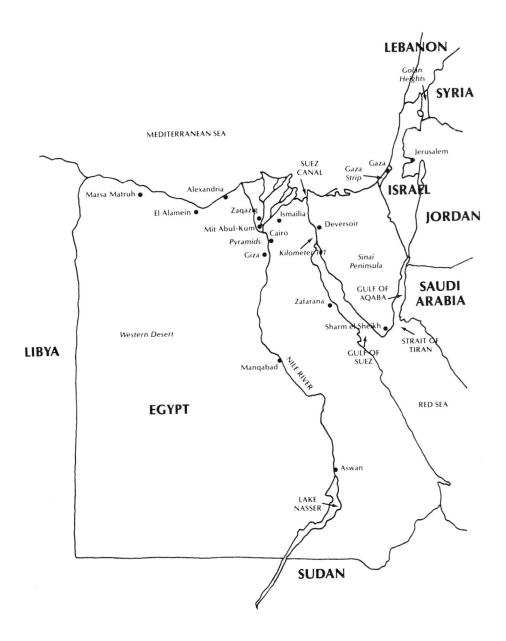

Anwar el-Sadat

A Man of Peace

by Deborah Nodler Rosen

 CHILDRENS PRESS ®
CHICAGO

ACKNOWLEDGMENTS

The author wishes to acknowledge with appreciation the assistance of Essam Elessawi, Vice Consul, Consulate General of the Arab Republic of Egypt, Chicago, Illinois; Mohamed Hakki, official spokesperson for the government of the Arab Republic of Egypt and former chairman of the State Information Service under President Anwar el-Sadat; Carl F. Petry, associate professor of history, Northwestern University; Camelia Sadat, author of *My Father and I*, Macmillan Publishing Company, New York.

PICTURE ACKNOWLEDGMENTS

Egyptian State Information Service—Frontispiece
United Press International, Inc.—pages 8, 20, 60 (bottom), 61 (bottom), 106
AP/Wide World Photos—pages 44, 59 (2 photos), 60 (top), 61 (top), 62, 63 (2 photos), 64, 65 (2 photos), 66, 78, 94, 119
Horizon Graphics—maps on pages 1, 39, 56, 93
Cover illustration by Len W. Meents

Library of Congress Cataloging in Publication Data

Rosen, Deborah Nodler.
   Anwar el-Sadat: a man of peace.

   Includes index.
   Summary: A biography of the Egyptian president who won the Nobel peace prize for his efforts in ending Arab-Israeli conflict.
   1. Sadat, Anwar, 1918-1981—Juvenile literature.
2. Egypt—Presidents—Biography—Juvenile literature.
3. Egypt—History—1919-   —Juvenile literature.
4. Egypt—Foreign relations—Israel—Juvenile literature.
5. Israel—Foreign relations—Egypt—Juvenile literature.
[1. Sadat, Anwar, 1918-1981. 2. Egypt—Presidents.
3. Nobel prizes—Biography] I. Title.
DT107.828.S23R67   1986   962'.054'0924 [B] [92]   86-9541
ISBN 0-516-03214-3

Table of Contents

INTRODUCTION

The midday sun flashed on the Star of Sinai and the other medals that Anwar el-Sadat, the president of Egypt, wore proudly on his blue uniform and the bright green sash adorning it. Firecrackers exploded above him. Cannons bombarded the air, sending out tiny parachutes weighed down with Egyptian flags and pictures of the president. Blaring music and the boom of drums drowned out the noisy crowd at this victory parade. The date was October 6, 1981.

Eight years before, almost to the hour, President Sadat had launched a war. Israel had been the enemy. Recapturing the Sinai desert, which separated the two countries, had been his aim. Egypt had fought three previous wars with Israel, losing territory to the Israelis each time. President Sadat believed there could be no peace with Israel until Egypt had regained its lost land. Peace was his goal, he said, and in the search for peace, eveything was permissible—including war.

The fighting had gone on for more than two weeks. Young men who dreamed of growing fig trees and oranges died instead in fiery tank explosions. Both sides wept for their dead and for the lives that could never be repaired. Both nations reeled from the terrible losses they endured. Yet both claimed victory.

Every year President Sadat celebrated that victory on October 6. He also used that victory as a stepping-stone. He did what no Arab leader had ever done before. He went to Jerusalem, the capital city of Israel, and embraced his enemies. Later, he and Menachem Begin, prime minister of Israel, journeyed to the United States where they held talks and eventually signed a peace treaty.

That peace had continued. The menacing tanks and field guns now rumbling past held no ammunition. The president puffed on his pipe as he gazed up at the jet fighters streaking white, yellow, and red trails of smoke across the sapphire sky. He smiled, knowing his daring actions had made this parade possible.

President Sadat did not notice that one truck had stopped short directly in front of him. He paid no attention as other vehicles braked and swerved around it. Suddenly bullets crashed into the reviewing stand. First one soldier, then three more rushed toward the podium shouting, "Glory for Egypt!" The president rose as if to salute. The soldiers aimed their gunfire at the medals on the blue uniform. Sadat, mortally wounded, slumped forward. Thirty seconds ticked by before anybody came to his aid. As at other turning points in his life, Sadat was alone. The assassination took less than a minute. Why would anyone want to kill the man who, after four wars in thirty years, had brought peace to Egypt?

Chapter 1

A CHILD OF THIS LAND

The top of the oven was Anwar's favorite resting place. The huge oven, built from mud bricks, took up most of the space in the cooking room at the back of his tiny house. He lived in the Egyptian village of Mit Abul-Kum, forty miles northwest of Cairo. Anwar liked to spread a mat over the wide, flat top of the oven. He'd stretch out there with his younger brothers and the family rabbits and wait eagerly for his mother or grandmother to tell him bedtime stories.

They did not fill his head with tales of romance or make-believe. Anwar listened night after night to the dramas of real-life heroes. He loved the ballad of Zahran best. Zahran, a farmer, had lived in a village just three miles from Mit Abul-Kum. He was a hero to the Sadat family because he fought the British who had been in control of Egypt since 1882. Before Anwar was old enough to understand Egypt's centuries of suffering under foreign rule, "I knew," he said, "that there were forces, called 'the British,' who were alien to us, and that they were evil."[1]

In the Zahran story, British officers were out shooting pigeons. By accident, one of their shots hit a grain silo and set it ablaze. The local peasant farmers burst into a fury

9

when they saw the flames. They came running to save the precious wheat. There was a fight, and a British soldier was killed. The British arrested the farmers. They were put on trial and four were condemned to death by hanging. Zahran was the first to die. He held his head high as he walked toward the scaffold. Zahran was proud, Sadat's grandmother explained, because he stood up to his enemies. "I listened to that ballad night after night," Anwar said. "I often saw Zahran and lived his heroism in dream and reverie—I wished *I* were Zahran."[2]

Second best to being Zahran was sharing the story with his village friends. Anwar's earliest and happiest memories were of his village and his grandmother. "Everything in the village . . . made me ineffably happy: going out to get carrots, not from the green grocer's but from the land itself; slipping an onion in to roast in our oven (while the family baked bread), then taking it out at sundown to eat; our boyish games in the village by moonlight."[3]

Anwar's grandmother took charge of the Sadat children during their years in Mit Abul-Kum. Their father, Muhammad, worked as a clerk for the Egyptian army. He was stationed far away in the Sudan, an African country south of Egypt where Anwar's mother had been born. Anwar had inherited her dark skin and tightly curled black hair. Since his parents were away many months of the year, his grandmother supervised the farm work on their 2½-acre plot.

"How I loved that woman!"[4] Anwar said. When they heard the village crier shouting, "the treacle has arrived,"[5] his grandmother would rush outside pulling Anwar with her. What excitement as they hurried to buy a jar of the sweet syrupy treacle from the ship docked in the canal. What happiness as he padded barefoot beside her in his long Arab dress, thinking about the delicious treat that awaited him.

~ Villagers greeted his grandmother with great respect. That pleased Anwar. She was the one who knew not only the ancient Arab remedies for illness, but the latest news from the countryside too. And she was religious, following the teaching of the Koran—the holy book of her Muslim religion. It contained the word of God as revealed to the prophet Muhammad. Anwar learned the duties of prayer and fasting. "*Sheikh*" (religious leader) his friends nicknamed him because he was so dedicated. He developed a dark callus called a prayer knot on his forehead from touching it to the ground in worship five separate times each day.

His grandmother raised him on her special blend of patriotism and religion—love of Egypt and love of God. "Nothing is as significant as your being a child of this land," she told him. "Land is immortal, for it harbors the mysteries of creation."[6] Anwar experienced the mystical tie that Egyptians through the ages have felt toward their land and the Nile, the life-giving river that runs through it.

Anwar's Egypt can be described in two colors: green and

brown. The Nile, like an odd-shaped tree with a long trunk, cuts a deep, green path from Egypt's southern border to the Mediterranean Sea. Along the banks of the river, the land blossoms green and fertile. But the rest of Egypt—95 percent—is brown, barren, uninhabitable desert.

The Nile gave life and taught Anwar's ancestors, the ancient Egyptians, how to survive through cooperation and organization. Once each year the Nile overflows its banks. The torrents of water come from the spring rains that pour into the river at its sources deep within Africa. Villagers had to plan and work together distributing the floodwater over the parched fields. Without it no crop could grow. Those ancient Egyptians learned their lessons of cooperation and organization so well that four thousand years before the birth of Christ, Egypt had a magnificent civilization. Great pharaohs ruled one after the other for centuries. The symbols of their civilization—monumental pyramids, the Sphinx, tombs filled with golden furniture and rare perfumes—were all made possible by the richness of the Nile valley.

Little had changed since the pharaohs ruled. The floodwater reached Mit Abul-Kum in the cold days of December, as it always had. But before Anwar was born, the British had repaired and enlarged the dams and canals built to control the flooding. The special canal near Mit Abul-Kum was filled to overflowing for just two weeks. Villagers had to water every field in that time. No one could do the job alone.

Anwar remembered walking to the canal at dawn. He joined the other villagers working the *tunbur*, or Archimedes' screw, as their ancestors had done. The *tunbur* was a long tube with a spiral inside. One end went in the water. Then, as someone turned it, water twisted up the spiral and spilled out the top of the tube. Some in Anwar's village owned *tunburs*; others did not. They all shared.

Years later, Anwar still remembered how he felt. "That kind of collective work—with and for other men, with no profit or any kind of individual reward . . . made me feel that I belonged not merely to my immediate family at home, or even to the big family of the village, but to something vaster and more significant: the land."[7]

Although Anwar's grandmother never learned to read, education was all-important to her. Her son (Anwar's father) was the first in the village to graduate from elementary school. This achievement earned him the title *effendi*, meaning educated man.

Anwar was expected to follow in his father's footsteps. His grandmother sent him to the Koranic Teaching School where he learned to read and write Arabic and memorize all 114 chapters of the Koran. "I remember," he said, "how I sat among my fellow students on the floor, holding a writing tablet and a reed pen, my only tools of learning. My Arab dress had a large, deep pocket which I used to fill up in the morning with dry cheese and bread crusts, and from which

I would snatch mouthfuls during our lessons."[8] Anwar's grandmother later sent him to a Coptic (Christian) school. He learned enough English there to speak with a British soldier who visited the school.

In 1925, when Anwar was seven, his father returned from the Sudan and moved the family to Cairo. The giant city teemed with people. Anwar missed the village, with its mud huts, donkeys grazing in the sun, and mulberry trees for climbing. Cairo even smelled different—faintly rotten, like garbage. Gone was the scent of jasmine and the odor of fresh-cut hay. The Sadats crowded into a tiny four-room apartment. The family grew until Anwar was sharing the space with twelve brothers and sisters. At this time Anwar first learned that he had been born on December 25, 1918. In the village no special notice had been paid to his birthday.

In Cairo, Anwar found new reasons to hate the British. He resented the way they looked down on everything Egyptian as inferior, just because it wasn't Western and European. He often wondered what had brought these foreigners to his city. Egyptians had been asking the same question since Biblical times, as waves of invaders—Persians, Greeks, Romans—conquered their ancient land. In A.D. 642, Egypt fell to the Muslims, the followers of Islam, which means "surrender." Believers surrendered to the will of God, whom they called Allah. Most Egyptians adopted Islam and the Arabic language. Other foreigners including Mamelukes

14

and Turks ruled in the centuries that followed.

Anwar's grandmother painted vivid pictures of foreign injustice as she described the digging of the Suez Canal. Egyptians with picks and shovels had hacked away a hundred-mile-long trench in the desert. Under the relentless sun and their superiors' whips, they cut a path so that European ships from the Mediterranean could sail directly into the Red Sea, instead of detouring around the huge continent of Africa. So many died of disease and hunger, it was claimed that "the Canal was built on the skulls of Egyptians."

But for all their suffering, Egyptians did not reap the benefits. The French and British owned the company that collected the fees. The Suez Canal Company, a French company, began digging the canal in 1859 and completed it in 1869. The khedive (the foreign ruler) of Egypt had shares in the canal. But when Egypt faced bankruptcy in 1875, Britain bought the khedive's shares.

Finally in 1881 Ahmed Arabi, an Egyptian soldier, wanted to throw out the foreign rulers. Shouting, "Egypt for the Egyptians," he led ten thousand ragtag troops against the khedive. Anwar's grandmother had not known Arabi personally, but her uncle had. Arabi's efforts to free Egypt had inspired her patriotism. Arabi's efforts had also inspired Great Britain's fear because the British did not want to lose control of the Suez Canal.

Great Britain landed thirty thousand soldiers who defeated

Arabi's forces. Not only did Arabi's fight for independence fail to overthrow the khedive, it also brought the British to Egypt. Their troops kept the khedive on the throne, insisting in return that he take British "advice" and protect British interests. Demands for independence grew. Anwar's family was proud of those Egyptians who led a second rebellion against the British in 1919.

The British did not want to give up Egypt, which sat at the crossroads between the West and the East, Africa and Asia. They took a new approach. In 1922 Britain granted Egypt independence and a constitution and made a younger brother of the khedive, named Fuad I, king of Egypt. Britain's goal was to rule indirectly through pro-British politicians. Great Britain, when its policy was not followed, pressured King Fuad into dissolving the Egyptian parliament and setting aside the 1923 constitution. To make matters worse, the British treated Egyptians like second-class citizens in their own land. Many agreed with Anwar that the British were evil.

Anwar's new school was near one of King Fuad's palaces. In spring, luscious apricots hung from the trees in the royal orchard. Anwar and his friends looked longingly at them. Did they dare? Taking the king's possessions could mean death. Hearts pounding at the risk, they helped themselves to the fruit. Anwar was willing to take great chances for what he wanted.

In 1930, after Anwar and his older brother, Tal'at, graduated from primary school, their father enrolled them in secondary school. Education was not free. Their combined tuition payment equaled their father's salary for an entire month. Tal'at disliked school. He took the money for the second installment and ran off on a wild spree. "Perhaps destiny decreed this," Anwar thought. His father could not have continued both payments. As the second son, Anwar would probably have lost out.

Mr. Sadat had difficulty supporting his large family. Bread was homemade because they could not afford to buy it at the bakery. Anwar's classmates wore elegant suits and had money for expensive chocolates and candy. He had one old suit and his allowance was two *millimes* a day—just enough for a cup of milky tea.

One afternoon Anwar went to buy matches, which he pronounced "mutches." The customers in the store laughed at his pronunciation. "You must ask for *matches*, not mutches," they explained. As they teased "I became more obstinate," Anwar said. "Who did they think they were? . . . They believed that superiority belongs only to the rich . . . [but] in the village . . . a man of integrity was the ideal, whatever his poverty."[9]

Poverty was not Anwar's only problem. His second-year examination grade was low and his school urged him to study for it again. Anwar, in a spirit of challenge, refused.

He enrolled in another school, but eventually failed the examination for a General Certificate of Education (G.C.E.). "That result was a turning point in my life. I realized that my failure was a sign. God was not satisfied with me, perhaps because of my negligence, perhaps because of my overconfidence."[10] Feeling guilty and determined to repent, Anwar transferred to another school and finally earned his G.C.E.

During these years, Egyptian resentment of the British was growing and Anwar joined student demonstrators. They entered the school kitchen and smashed plates. Then they rushed onto the street, overturned a streetcar and set it on fire as they shouted for the 1923 constitution. "But I didn't even know what that Constitution really was,"[11] he said.

Mahatma Gandhi was leading the fight against the British in India. Anwar admired this man who went on hunger strikes and wore a simple white cloth instead of Western clothing. When Gandhi came to Egypt in 1932, Anwar imitated him. He stripped to the waist and sat in a corner of their roof spinning yarn like Gandhi. The air was frigid. Finally his father convinced him that his efforts were not helping Egypt in its fight for independence. All he would gain was a case of pneumonia.

In 1936, Great Britain and Egypt signed a treaty that permitted Egypt to expand the size of its army. Now Anwar was eligible to join the Royal Military Academy—if he had the right connections. But the Sadats of Mit Abul-Kum didn't know anyone wealthy or with a high enough rank to have a title such as pasha. Then Anwar's father remembered a friend who worked for a pasha connected with the Military Academy. The friend arranged for Anwar and his father to stand in the hallway of the pasha's palace. They hoped the nobleman would speak to them. As the pasha rushed by, the friend pointed to the Sadats. "Oh, yes. You're the senior clerk of the Health Department and that's your son who . . . I see . . . all right, all right!"[12] The pasha spoke haughtily as he dashed through the door. Anwar never forgot how angry and humiliated he felt at this arrogant treatment. He did, however, win one of the fifty-two places at the Royal Military Academy.

Egypt's King Farouk and American President Franklin D. Roosevelt met aboard an American warship in 1945.

Chapter 2

DREAM OF INDEPENDENCE

A campfire blazed in the Egyptian desert at the foot of Mount el-Cherif. Hours before, the desert had blazed with heat. But now with the sun gone and the sky black, the young soldiers who talked so intently needed the campfire for heat as well as light.

In 1938, few people beyond that circle of firelight had ever heard those young men's names. Egyptians followed their daily chores unaware that in Manqabad, a dusty army garrison in Upper Egypt, soldiers talked about revolution. Such talk was treason and the standard punishment was death. Anwar el-Sadat was one of those soldiers.

Sadat was stationed at Manqabad after his graduation from the Royal Military Academy. There he met other officers who shared his dangerous dream of forcing the British out of Egypt. Gamal Abdel Nasser impressed Sadat most. Nasser stood six feet tall and ramrod straight. He was more serious than the others. When he spoke he said things like, "The country has fallen into chaos. Freedom is our natural right. The way lies before us—revolution."[1]

Sadat led discussions about Egypt's history. He had read more than the others. On Thursdays when an army bus took the men to a nearby town, they looked for entertainment or rushed off to the movies. Sadat preferred to sit in the cafe and read books he had ordered by mail or purchased at secondhand shops in Cairo.

Nasser and Sadat organized the army officers into a secret revolutionary society, later called the Free Officers. Their goal was to get rid of King Fuad's son Farouk who had inherited the throne. They also wanted to take over the Egyptian government, which Sadat said was just a puppet of the English who pulled the strings. Even though the Parliament and the 1923 constitution had been restored and an Anglo-Egyptian Treaty had been signed in 1936, Britain was still the power behind the throne and Parliament. In addition, British troops remained to protect their interests—particularly the Suez Canal. Sadat was quick to point out that Egypt wasn't really independent.

During this time, Sadat met another group of Egyptians called the Muslim Brotherhood who also wanted to expel the British. Sadat wondered if the officers and the Brotherhood could work together, but he discovered they had different goals.

The officers wanted to restore Egypt's pride by improving its standard of living using Western industry, science, and technology. Then, independently, Egypt could prosper in the twentieth century. The Brotherhood believed Western culture was destroying Egypt. It wanted to turn its back on the

West and create a "pure" society based on the religious teachings of Islam.

Among Egypt's Muslims it was customary to marry young. Sadat chose Ekbal Madi, the daughter of the *omdah*, or head-man, of Mit Abul-Kum, as his bride. Sadat had been friendly with the Madi family from childhood. Ekbal's brother had saved Anwar from drowning in the canal. After the Sadats moved to Cairo, Anwar often stayed with the Madi family during his summers at Mit Abul-Kum. The wedding, a tradi-tional three-day celebration, took place in November 1940. On the first day Ekbal and Anwar signed the marriage con-tract. On the second and third days the bride cooked a special meal for her husband while other women prepared a feast for the rest of the family and guests. The marriage photo showed Anwar tall and imposing in his army uniform. Ekbal, her dark eyes solemn, wore a long white dress and lace veil. Later, in Cairo, the Sadat family prepared a room in their house for the young couple while Anwar was in the army.

Anwar continued recruiting officers, but he and Egypt were about to be caught up in World War II. In Germany, Adolf Hitler had grandiose plans for conquering the world. Austria and Czechoslovakia were the first countries to fall. Next Hitler's expertly trained Nazi troops marched into Poland. Great Britain declared war on Germany on Sep-tember 3, 1939. So did France. Italy was in league with Germany. World War II had begun.

Britain had to defend its empire—all the countries and colonies that owed allegiance to the British Crown. One fourth of the world and its population was part of that empire, or Commonwealth, as it was now called. Casualty figures rose daily as British soldiers fought the Germans in snow, sand, and jungles around the world. Britain was getting desperate. Where could it find enough soldiers to defend the vital Suez Canal?

Italy had declared war on Britain in June 1940. The following winter British troops were winning battles against the Italians in the North African territory west of Egypt. Hitler sent two German divisions under the command of General Erwin Rommel to help the Italians. In a daring attack, Rommel sent the British reeling back.

Sadat, like most Egyptians, did not want to fight for the British, whom they hated. They wanted Egypt to remain neutral and not become a battlefield between two enemy nations. Nonetheless, Britain had ordered Egyptian troops to help defend the Western Desert, the sandy wasteland on the western border. Sadat had been posted with Egyptian army units to Marsa Matruh on the Mediterranean Sea. Egyptians were enraged. Crowds chanted, "We have nothing to do with that war."[2] The Egyptian Parliament was pro-German. It adopted a policy of "saving Egypt from the scourge of war."[3]

British troops failed twice to recapture the North African

territory. Rommel's tanks were poised on Egypt's frontier. Great Britain got panicky, afraid that Egyptian troops stationed in the Western Desert might turn and attack British soldiers instead of the Nazis. London ordered all Egyptian units to leave the Western Desert and turn in their weapons. Sadat was furious at this humiliation. Why should an English prime minister give orders to the Egyptian army? He convinced his fellow officers to disobey them. If the British wanted the weapons, they would have to take them by force. The British quickly backed down and, still armed, Sadat and his men marched toward Cairo.

Here was the chance he had been waiting for. Britain's position in the Middle East was collapsing. Sadat believed his troops could enter Cairo and throw them out. He urged the retreating Egyptian army units to rise in revolt, and eagerly made plans for the revolution. "I felt very happy,"[4] he said.

Sadat led his men to the spot where all the troops had agreed to assemble. They waited, discussed their plans, washed their vehicles, and waited some more. Not a single other unit joined them. "Thus the first plan I laid down for a revolution came to grief,"[5] Sadat admitted. But he had no intention of giving up. If Egyptian troops could not oust the British themselves, he'd ask the Germans for help. But he didn't want Germany to replace the British and control Egypt. What he wanted was independence.

Many Egyptians were pro-German, including Egypt's army chief, General Aziz al-Masri. When the British forced his dismissal, Sadat offered to help him escape from Egypt to meet the Germans. The general's plane crashed on takeoff. He wasn't injured, but the British caught and arrested him. They knew of Sadat's friendship with al-Masri, so they arrested Sadat too.

Sadat faced a jail term if the prosecutor linked him with the general's attempt to meet the Germans. Sadat was brought to headquarters early in the morning, but the cross-examination didn't begin until midnight. The prosecutor hammered away with question after question. Sadat, assured and calm, answered each one. He was careful to reveal no incriminating evidence. Finally the prosecutor released him. Sadat had an unexpected reaction. He felt awe and respect for the British legal system. He realized that in other countries, there would have been no legal proceedings. He would have been thrown against a wall and shot, especially in wartime. But the British would not take away his liberty without clear proof he had committed a crime. Would the Germans have acted similarly? In his autobiography Sadat wrote, "That shows, I thought . . . the advantages of the rule of the law."[6]

Great Britain suffered more defeats during the summer of 1942. German troops, led by Rommel, marched across Egypt. As Egyptians shouted, "Advance Rommel," Sadat and the Free Officers saw a chance to bargain for Egypt's freedom. They agreed to offer the Germans their fighting services and photographs of British positions in exchange for Egyptian independence.

While Sadat searched for a way to get this treaty information to Rommel, two Nazi spies contacted him. They had counterfeit bank notes and two radio transmitters to send messages back to the German command. Sadat hid his activities carefully. The German spies, however, set up headquarters on a Nile houseboat owned by an Egyptian dancer and stocked with bottles of whiskey and perfume. They also spent a good deal of time and money at the Kit Kat Night Club, where British Intelligence noticed them. Sadat did not realize they were being watched. He went to their houseboat to borrow one transmitter and took it to his father's house where he was living.

That night there was a loud knock at the door. Sadat's sister, Sekina, recalled, "British troops and King Farouk's political police came crashing into our house, hurling us out of our beds, breaking furniture and crockery, tearing the place to pieces. . . . They were looking for Anwar."[7] Even though his brother, Tal'at, managed to conceal the transmitter, Sadat was arrested.

For three days and nights, Sadat ate nothing, as his mind searched for a way out. He didn't know that Winston Churchill himself, Great Britain's prime minister, had come to

Egypt in secrecy to bolster his troops' morale. Churchill interviewed the two German spies and promised to spare their lives in exchange for a complete confession.

As a result of their testimony, Sadat was stripped of his army rank and sent to the Alien's Jail. "The image of Zahran rose before my eyes almost visibly all the way to the Alien's Jail. I saw him advancing toward death with his head held high, happy at what he had done. At last I had achieved what Zahran had done before me. . . . I was overwhelmed by a strange joy—the joy of acknowledging a vast inner strength which I alone recognized."[8]

Sadat spent the next two years in various jails. He used the time to his advantage. He asked for English books to improve his knowledge of that language. Later he met a German prisoner who agreed to teach him German. They began translating a novel. At first Sadat struggled hard to understand four lines during his lesson. Seven months later, he could complete an entire chapter in the same amount of time. Eventually Sadat became fluent in both English and German.

The war continued through 1944. The Germans lost several major battles. As British fortunes improved, they released some Egyptian prisoners, but not Sadat. He decided to escape, and staged a hunger strike. When he was transferred to a hospital, he arranged for a friend to drive up at lunchtime, the busiest part of the day. Breaking away from his guard, he jumped into the waiting car and within minutes was in the hideout his friends had prepared.

Sadat lived as a fugitive from October 1944 until September 1945. He grew a beard, changed his name, and tried to support his family by working at odd jobs. But there was never enough money. For Sadat, poverty led to tragedy. He was a father now. His first child, a daughter, Rokaya, had been born in September 1941. His second daughter, Rawia, died. She caught a fever but there was no money for a doctor, medicine, or even sugar to sweeten and enrich her drinking water and help prevent dehydration. Sadat suffered the anguish of all parents unable to aid their child.

Finally the war ended. Germany was defeated and peace returned. Britain ended martial law—the wartime laws under which Sadat had been convicted. Again, thanks to the British system of justice, Anwar el-Sadat was a free man.

But Egypt was not a free country. Sadat thought violence was the best way to pressure the British into leaving. He wanted to blow up the British embassy. When Nasser refused, Sadat joined others who approved of his schemes. Together they decided to attack important Egyptian leaders who were pro-British. They wanted to make it very clear that it was no longer safe to serve Great Britain. Sadat chose Mustafa el-Nahas Pasha as victim number one. As Egypt's wartime prime minister, el-Nahas had supported British policy. That made him a traitor in Sadat's eyes.

Sadat had taught his team of revolutionaries to use hand grenades. They picked a young man named Hussein Tewfik for the task. El-Nahas was scheduled to make a speech. As his car inched along the teeming street, Sadat and the others took up their positions. Police scanned the crowd for troublemakers. With a swift motion, Tewfik hurled the grenade. It missed by six seconds. Splinters struck a bus of British army women.

The revolutionaries met at a nearby cafe to plan their next step. They decided to get rid of Amin Osman Pasha because they believed he was a traitor too. Again, Tewfik was the assassin; again Sadat waited nearby. "Pasha, Pasha," Tewfik called, as he pulled the trigger with deadly accuracy. An Egyptian air force officer was passing by. Later, he identified Tewfik, who confessed to the murder. Sadat did not have long to wait that dark night in January, before there was a knock at the door, a search, and an arrest. Tewfik had described Sadat's part in the action.

Back in Alien's Jail, Sadat tried to upset the case against him. He sent telegrams falsely accusing the prison governor of torturing him. He threatened to go on a hunger strike. Finally the prosecuting attorney transferred Sadat to Cairo's Central Prison, cell 54.

Water oozed from the cell walls; bugs crawled everywhere. There was no bed, no table, no chair, no lamp. Furnishings consisted of one thin mat, and a blanket too filthy to touch. This was to be Sadat's home for eighteen months. The Alien's Jail, with electricity and edible food, suddenly seemed luxurious. Now in January 1946, Sadat faced a year and a half in solitary confinement, without pencil, paper, radio, or books. The difference in prisons seemed symbolic of everything that was wrong with Egypt. Even the jail for foreigners was better than the jail for ordinary Egyptians.

During that summer while Sadat was in prison, Ekbal gave birth to another daughter also named Rawia, after the child who had died.

Sadat came to know himself in cell 54. He wrote, "Two places in this world make it impossible for a man to escape from himself: a battlefield and a prison cell. In Cell 54 I could only be my own companion, day and night, and it was only natural that I should come to know that 'self' of mine."[9]

One problem Sadat had to face was his marriage. He realized that he had nothing in common with his wife and he suffered with that knowledge. Then in cell 54 his path became clear to him. He decided that divorce was the only solution.

"Nothing is more important than self-knowledge. Once I had come to know what I wanted, and got rid of what I didn't, I was reconciled to my 'self' and learned to live at peace with it. . . . My relations with the entire universe began to be reshaped, and love became the fountainhead of all my actions. . . . I cannot bring myself to hate anybody, as I am by nature committed to love. This became quite clear to me through suffering and pain, in Cell 54."[10] Once Sadat understood his "self," he felt free and at peace. "This is why I regard my last eight months in prison as the happiest period of my life,"[11] he said.

After two years in prison, Sadat's case finally came to trial. The guards wanted to take the prisoners to court in handcuffs. Sadat vigorously objected, claiming he had not yet been convicted. The guards backed down. Many Egyptians rallied to Sadat's support and hired the best lawyers for him and his conspirators. If convicted, Sadat faced the death penalty, or hard labor for life. As the trial progressed, Sadat helped throw the case into confusion during the cross-examination. The defendants' contradictory stories further weakened it. Finally in July 1948, the verdict came down. Sadat was found not guilty.

Chapter 3

EGYPT WILL GREET OUR MOVEMENT WITH HOPE AND WITH JOY

Where to now? Sadat pondered, after his release from cell 54. He looked at what he had gained and lost in prison. He understood himself. He knew the power of love and the danger of acting from fear. But he had lost his army commission. He had no career, no money, no job, and it seemed, no future.

However, his friend, Hassan Izzat, hadn't forgotten him. Izzat suddenly appeared in the doorway, as Sadat finished his morning prayer. One look around the dingy, rundown room and Izzat said, "Let's go . . . to where I live, in Suez."[1] One glance at Sadat's only clothes, a limp white jacket and threadbare gray trousers, convinced Izzat to buy him new ones.

Once in Suez, Sadat realized Izzat hadn't acted just from friendship. He did business with Saudi Arabians and wanted Sadat, hero of the assassination, to impress them. Sadat thought his presence had helped Izzat make some deals and calculated his own share to be 180 sovereigns. But Izzat paid him only 60 and kept the rest.

Late one evening when Sadat returned to the Suez house,

he came face-to-face with a stunning green-eyed, black-haired young girl. "I was eating mango and suddenly, he was in front of me. I went running away,"[2] Jihan Raouf said. Jihan was a cousin of Izzat's wife. She was immediately attracted to Sadat because of his personality and revolutionary activities. Jihan had a revolutionary streak herself.

In traditional Muslim households, women were trained to be subservient. Not Jihan. Her father, Safwat Raouf, raised his two sons and his two daughters as well to be self-reliant individuals. Gladys, Jihan's mother, was English, which explained why Jihan called her father "Daddy."

In traditional Muslim households, family honor depended on the pure reputation of the women, for whom education was not important. Young girls stayed safely at home. Not Jihan. She attended a Christian missionary girls' school from the time she was four to age twelve. She continued her education at a secondary school in Cairo.

In traditional Muslim households, marriages were financial arrangements based on money and status. Daughters married the man their parents chose. Not Jihan. Anwar el-Sadat was penniless, his army career was over, and his family lacked prestige. He was not even handsome. None of that mattered to fifteen-year-old Jihan. She had fallen in love.

Jihan's mother was shocked by Sadat's dark skin and his prison record. She rejected him as an unacceptable suitor.

But for Jihan, the outer trappings were immaterial. She saw the inner man, his courage, and his dedication to Egypt.

Sadat proposed to Jihan on September 29, 1948. Jihan's wishes prevailed and her father accepted the proposal for his daughter. They were married on May 29, 1949, Jihan resplendent in a white lace gown. The young couple moved into a modest hotel in Zaqaziq where Sadat was working on a business project for Izzat.

The two men had contracted to supply drinking water to nearby villages. At last here was a chance to earn money so he could set up a permanent apartment with Jihan and fulfill his obligations to the daughters from his first marriage. He now had three; Rokaya, Rawia, and Camelia. He worked fifteen to seventeen hours a day to earn the money quickly. After six months at this backbreaking schedule, they had made a profit. Anwar asked for his share and was amazed when Izzat claimed Sadat had already drawn most of it. Sadat knew this was an outright lie. He was shocked and saddened by his friend's conduct.

"All I wanted was to get away,"[3] Sadat said. He had very little money when he left Zaqaziq. But he knew he had lost a great deal more than money. He felt that during his arguments over his share of the profits, he had lost the "self" he had discovered in cell 54. It was time to find that "self" again.

Sadat decided the army was the link to his dream. Since

he had been acquitted, the army was free to reinstate him. Sadat asked some friends to use their influence. On January 15, 1950, Anwar el-Sadat was an army captain once more.

Gamal Abdel Nasser was the first to congratulate him. Since Sadat's arrest in 1942, Nasser had been working secretly to increase the number of Free Officers. There were Free Officers now throughout the army. Nasser had organized them into groups called cells. Members of one cell never knew the identity of any others. That way if one cell was discovered, membership could not be traced beyond the single group.

The Free Officer groups were growing so rapidly that by 1951 Nasser set up a council to run them. Sadat was one of the original members. This constituent council had three goals: to remove the British from Egyptian soil; to remove the extravagant King Farouk from the Egyptian throne; and to establish a republic.

At the same time that opposition to Egypt's playboy king was growing, dramatic events were taking place in the Middle East. On May 14, 1948, the state of Israel came into existence. On the same day five Arab armies set out to destroy it. King Farouk sent one of those armies.

Israel had been created from territory called Palestine on the east coast of the Mediterranean Sea. Arabs and Jews both claimed that Palestine belonged to them. The Jews declared that God had promised the land to Abraham and his descendants. The Jews had conquered the local tribes and established a kingdom. King David set the capital in Jerusalem about 1000 B.C. and King Solomon built the temple there in the next century. The Romans destroyed both the temple and the kingdom in A.D. 70 and drove out most of the Jews.

Arabs, also claiming descent from Abraham, came into Palestine during the seventh century. These followers of Islam conquered the local peoples and converted them, just as they had done in Egypt. But the Arabs never established an independent nation. Like the Egyptians, they were governed by a series of foreign rulers. There were about twenty-five thousand Jews living in Palestine. Then in the 1880s, Jews from Europe began to arrive. Most were escaping from anti-Semitic persecution and dreamed of reestablishing a Jewish nation. These Zionists, as they were called, set up farming communities.

Britain, through an agreement in 1916, got control of Palestine during World War I. Soon after, the British government issued the Balfour Declaration, favoring the creation of a Jewish "national homeland" in Palestine. The League of Nations approved the Balfour Declaration and in 1917 gave Britain a mandate (the authority) to govern Palestine.

The trickle of immigrants turned into a flood. The new arrivals built cities, staked out farms, and started small industries. Arabs from surrounding areas also came to

Palestine. The Arabs felt the Zionists were intruding on Arab land. They feared the Jews would displace them, and they organized anti-Jewish riots. Since the Zionists were considered Westerners, or Europeans, these riots were partly anti-West. Arab leaders pressured Britain to keep the Zionists out and Britain further limited the number of Jews allowed to settle.

After World War II, Jews who had survived the war and Hitler's concentration camps flocked to the Holy Land. Britain forced many away. Jews within Palestine thought the British had betrayed them and attacked British headquarters and army depots. Arabs insisted too many Jews were entering. Both sides started attacking each other and their English peacekeepers. Great Britain was caught between two opposing peoples. It gave up its no-win position and returned the mandate to the United Nations.

Great Britain asked the United Nations to settle the Palestine problem. In November 1947, the United Nations divided Palestine between Arab and Jew. The Jews accepted the decision, but the Arabs did not. The Jews named their new nation Israel and declared it an independent state. Arabs, to help the Palestinian Arabs, called for a *jihad*, a holy war, to destroy the new country. They attacked, beginning the first Arab-Israeli War.

King Farouk wanted to shift attention from all the money he was spending on lavish palaces and extravagant parties.

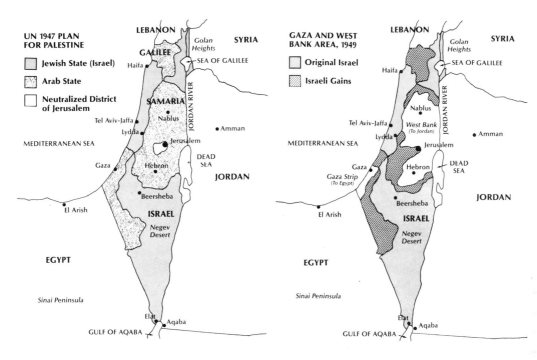

He hoped a quick victory for the Egyptian army would gain him popularity and respect. He sent his soldiers marching toward Israel. He even built a new boulevard so that when the army returned victorious it could parade into Cairo.

Sadat said, "The Egyptian forces entered the fight in great haste and confusion. . . . Our transport and medical services were poor, the food was terrible, heavy arms almost nonexistent. The only thing not in short supply was defective equipment—such as hand grenades which exploded in the hands of the throwers."[4] Sadat was appalled that, in the midst of this, King Farouk took the Engineer Corps away from the army and ordered it to build him a villa in Gaza.

Israel defeated the Arab armies, and gained more territory including West Jerusalem. The war "rocked the whole Arab world,"[5] Sadat said, and it was one of the causes of the Egyptian revolution. "The humiliation, frustration and anger aroused by the incompetence of the men who had led Egypt to defeat instead of victory, provoked a passionate desire to overthrow [the] regime."[6]

The majority of the army was still loyal to Farouk, their commander in chief. Nasser intended to start the revolution as soon as he had the support of enough Free Officers.

Egypt fell apart after the war. Sadat said it was one of the most unhappy periods in Egyptian history. He called it a "reign of terror." Young nationalists started riots demanding that Great Britain leave the Canal Zone. The British were equally determined to keep the zone and started searching any Egyptian entering or leaving the area. Egyptians were outraged at being searched on their own soil and increased their attacks. On January 25, 1952, British soldiers fired on Egyptian police, killing seventy.

Sadat described the day, called Black Saturday, which followed: "Mobs set fires to cafes, bars and cinemas. An army of idlers and trouble-makers . . . bore down on the center of the town. Gunsmiths' shops were broken into and looted. Barclay's Bank was set on fire. . . . Twelve people were killed at the Turf Club. Before night fell . . . the whole center of the town was ablaze."[7]

As for Egypt's leaders, Sadat reported angrily that Farouk

was giving a banquet, Prime Minister el-Nahas was having his nails manicured, and the minister of the interior was buying expensive furniture. When Farouk looked out from Abdin Palace and saw the wild mob rushing toward it, he called the army. Black Saturday was the last time it protected him.

Originally, Sadat said, the Free Officers planned the revolution for November 1955. After Black Saturday they advanced it to November 1952. Then Nasser discovered that the king's new war minister could identify some Free Officers and would probably arrest them. The revolution was pushed forward to July.

At a small desert outpost in the Sinai, Sadat received an urgent message. "Abou Menkar [Nasser's code name] asks you to leave for Cairo tomorrow. The revolution has been set to take place between July 22 and August 15."[8]

Sadat boarded a military train at 8:00 A.M. on July 22, and by 4:00 P.M. was chugging into Cairo. Before, Nasser had always been at the station waiting behind the wheel of his secondhand Austin. This time Nasser was nowhere in sight. Sadat assumed he was early. Since it was a lovely summer evening, he took Jihan to an outdoor movie.

Nasser had not gone to the station because he was preparing the Free Officers for the revolution that night. Farouk's spies had discovered their plans and posted guards around army headquarters. Nasser had to act quickly. He wanted to

41

take over without bloodshed. But he could not wait until the guards were withdrawn. By that time his men would be behind bars. He ordered the attack.

The soldiers inside headquarters did not want to die for Farouk. Should they follow orders, or follow their loyalties? Nasser's officers opened fire. Two defending soldiers fell. Inside, the commmanding officer went over to the rebels. The battle ended that quickly. Nasser, gun in hand, entered headquarters and arrested the army leaders who were loyal to Farouk. Other Free Officers took control of the remaining government buildings and the radio station. The revolution was a reality. Nasser was especially proud of the fact that only two Egyptian lives had been sacrificed to achieve it.

Meanwhile, Sadat was at the movies. When he returned home, he discovered that Nasser had been there twice and left a card saying, "Our project is on for tonight."⁹ Sadat was devastated. All those years of planning, the agony of prison, and now the revolution was taking place without him.

He drove at top speed to army headquarters and heard gunfire crackling in the air as he pulled up to the gate. An officer blocked his path, refusing to believe he was part of the revolutionary group. Finally one of the Free Officers heard his voice and came to his rescue. Only then did Sadat learn that army headquarters had fallen. He was filled with joy and went immediately to find Nasser.

Sadat felt honored when Nasser asked him to announce the revolution over the radio to the Egyptian people. He called Jihan, asking her to turn on the radio and listen. She heard Sadat say, "Egypt has lived through one of the darkest periods in its history. . . . Led by fools, traitors and incompetents, the Army was incapable of defending Egypt. . . . The Army is now in the hands of men in whose ability, integrity and patriotism you can have complete confidence. . . . Egypt will greet our Movement with hope and with joy. . . . May God sustain us!"[10]

Later, Sadat described the scene: "As I came out of the broadcasting station . . . I saw the streets . . . crowded with people. . . . Men, old and young, women and children, were kissing each other, shaking hands, coming together . . . all the time in total silence . . . the realization of their dream was beyond words; it was best expressed by this festive silence and by the feeling of togetherness which they all shared."[11]

The Free Officers controlled the country, but Farouk still sat on the throne. The Free Officers argued over the king's fate. Some called for exile; some called for execution. Nasser wanted to keep the revolution bloodless. He ordered tanks to surround the palace. Then he delivered an ultimatum to the king: leave the throne and the country by 6:00 P.M. on July 26. Farouk sailed from Egypt on the royal yacht at the designated time.

President Gamal Nasser, Vice-President Sadat, and Palestinian guerrilla leader Yassar Arafat (1970)

Chapter 4

IN NASSER'S SHADOW

Sadat looked with dismay at the Free Officers who assembled on July 27, 1952. Three days before, they had been simple soldiers sitting behind desks in Cairo. Now they held absolute power as members of the new Revolutionary Command Council. But their selfish quarreling disgusted Sadat. They cared more about which committees they would control than about Egypt.

Soon they were arguing over democracy versus dictatorship. Sadat defended dictatorship "from my eagerness to serve Egypt's interests—for what may be achieved 'democratically' in a year can be accomplished 'dictatorially' in a day."[1] Everyone agreed with Sadat except Nasser who voted for democracy. "I cannot accept this . . . opting for a dictatorship," Nasser shouted. "I hereby resign all my posts."[2] He turned on his heel and strode from the room.

"It was difficult for me then to grasp what Nasser was after,"[3] Sadat said. The inexperienced council needed Nasser, and asked him to come back and resume leadership. Suddenly Sadat understood that Nasser's talk about democracy was just a ploy. He had wanted to be dictator all along and had manipulated the council into making him one.

Within a year, the council, with Nasser as chairman, had suspended Egypt's constitution and abolished political parties. Nasser trusted no one. He had spies spying on other spies. "I have been a conspirator for so long that I mistrust all around me,"[4] he said. Newspaper and radio broadcasts were carefully censored. So were the mails. Nasser ordered hundreds of telephones tapped. No one felt safe speaking out. Anyone suspected of plotting against the government was put on trial, including hundreds from the Muslim Brotherhood. Their members had tried to overthrow the council and assassinate Nasser.

Nasser had said, "Show me ten men I can trust and I'll start delegating authority."[5] Sadat felt a great bond of respect for Nasser and was devastated when he discovered Nasser did not trust even him. Sadat claimed other council members were jealous of him because he had been a hero in the famous trial. He accused them of starting rumors that he was trying to grab power. Sadat realized, "If you showed ambition with Nasser, that was the end."[6] From then on he stayed in the background and avoided arguing with "the boss."

Sadat started a newspaper called *al Gumhuriah* (The Republic), which became the voice of the revolution. He wrote many articles attacking the United States and Israel. He was minister of state and also secretary-general of the Islamic Congress, which was organized to create strong ties among all Arab and Muslim countries. Later he was speaker of the National Assembly.

There were important events taking place in his private life too. Jihan gave birth to a daughter, Lubna. The following year, Sadat achieved the dream of all devout Muslims. He made a *hajj* (pilgrimage) to Mecca in Saudi Arabia, the holiest city in Islam. Under Islamic law, Muslims have five duties: they must declare their belief in one god, pray five times a day, give charity to the poor, fast from sunup to sundown during the sacred month of Ramadan, and make a *hajj* to Mecca. Like all pilgrims, Sadat donned a white cloth before praying at the *Ka'bah*, the dark stone structure that Muslims believe was built by Abraham and his son Ishmael.

Meanwhile, the Revolutionary Command Council turned its attention to Egypt's major problem of poverty. An employer paid more to hire a *gamoosa* (water buffalo) than to hire a *fellah* (Egyptian peasant). The council intended to change that using Western technology. It also cracked down on the pasha society of wealthy landlords who owned most of the fertile soil. Millions of Egyptians, like Sadat's family in Mit Abul-Kum, owned tiny farms or none at all. The council divided the larger estates among the peasants. Profits from the sale of the royal family's property went to build schools. Sadat found the rate breathtaking: three every two days. More schools were built in one year than in the previous twenty. Hospitals and clinics sprang up too.

Egypt became a republic in June 1953. To complete the revolution's goal of removing British troops from the Canal Zone, Nasser negotiated an evacuation agreement. When council members started bickering over the terms, Sadat called them stupid politicians. He finally convinced them to approve the document that, after seventy-five years, eliminated the last British soldiers from Egyptian soil.

Nasser faced other problems. He wanted to buy first-class military equipment from the United States with no strings attached. The United States refused to sell him any, and Nasser was furious. His soldiers stationed along the Israeli border were demanding better weapons.

Israel and Egypt had signed a cease-fire in 1949 after the first Arab-Israeli War. "Hostilities," as the actual fighting was called, had ended but hostility had not. When the war started, thousands of Palestinian Arabs were afraid to stay in Israeli territory. They left their homes and shops, and fled to the West Bank and Gaza areas that the United Nations had designated for the Palestinian state. But that state had never been formed. The king of Jordan annexed the West Bank, and Egypt kept control of Gaza. By the end of the war there were more than a half million refugees.

A guerrilla war started as some refugees raided Israeli villages, stole crops, and set land mines. Israelis fought back. Newspapers often contained articles describing the fighting:

> The Israeli Army patrol car wheeled south along the Gaza strip of enemy Egypt. A land mine exploded, killing three Israeli officers. An Israeli combat squad dynamited an Egyptian outpost in retaliation. Two days later, Egyptian and Israeli border guards waged a two-hour artillery duel.[7]

These clashes continued until Israeli troops wiped out thirty-nine Egyptian soldiers in a surprise attack. The Egyptians blamed their inferior weapons. Nasser called it a turning point and vowed retaliation.

"When America refused to buy my cotton or to sell me arms, I had to look elsewhere,"[8] Nasser said. He stunned the world by buying weapons from Czechoslovakia, a Communist country under Russian influence. He became an instant hero to the Arabs who demanded military action against Israel. However, even with Russian-made jet fighters and tanks, Nasser was not ready for war. Some of his soldiers lived in mud-brick huts. They had never turned on a light switch or driven a car. How could they operate anti-aircraft equipment without months of training?

Instead Nasser recruited Arab guerrillas called *fedayeen*, or "self-sacrificers," willing to die in hit-and-run attacks on Israel. Soon Egypt had seven hundred guerrillas in the Gaza Strip.

Like Sadat, Nasser recognized the urgency of improving Egypt's economy. His grand scale solution was to build a huge dam on the Nile at Aswan. The dam would create a lake (now called Lake Nasser) to hold floodwaters to be used for land irrigation. It would symbolize the greatness of modern Egypt, as the pyramids had in the ancient world. "It will give us an increase of 1.5 million [acres] of arable land," Nasser said, "and will provide us with about 2 billion kilowatts [of electricity]."[9]

Nasser was expecting great benefits from the Aswan High Dam and asked the United States, Great Britain, and the World Bank to finance it. They tentatively agreed. But in 1956 the United States and then Great Britain backed out. They opposed Nasser's friendship with Russia and did not think Egypt could afford Czech weapons and the dam too. An enraged Nasser shouted to the Americans, "You can kill yourselves."[10] He refused to be humiliated by the West again. If they wouldn't pay one way, they would pay another.

On July 26, 1956, Nasser announced to a multitude of cheering Egyptians that he had nationalized the Suez Canal. Its profits would finance the dam. "This money is ours and this Canal belongs to Egypt,"[11] he declared. At a prearranged signal in his speech army squads, guns drawn, moved into canal company offices.

Sadat was as shocked as the British and French who owned the company. Nasser had told him nothing. "If you had consulted me," he said, "I would have told you to be more careful. This step means war, and we're not ready for it."[12] Egyptians did not care. Nasser had erased seventy-four years of servitude in a single act. Britain and France called up troops. As England's prime minister declared, "The Egyptian had his thumb on our windpipe."[13] He also made clear, "Our quarrel is not with Egypt, still less with the Arab world—it is with Colonel Nasser."[14]

Nasser and the West squared off. Could Nasser prove that Egyptians were as efficient as Westerners at running the canal? Or would the allies, Britain and France, find an excuse for sending in soldiers? First the allies ordered their ships not to pay tolls to the new Egyptian company. Nasser let their ships through anyway. Then they ordered their canal ship pilots to leave. At least 179 of the 205 trained pilots were British and French, and they walked out.

Cameras from around the world focused on that hundred-mile trench in the earth, as Egyptians piloted the first convoy carefully along. And the second. And the third. All ships were sailing safely through—all but Israeli ships, which were forbidden.

Israel feared Egypt was preparing to attack. Why else had Nasser put the armies of Egypt, Jordan, and Syria under the command of one Egyptian general and bought all those Czech weapons? There were rumors that France, Britain, and Israel were holding secret meetings. Soon after,

Israeli troops sped across the Sinai toward the canal, and Britain and France bombed Egyptian air bases.

Britain, France, and Israel easily defeated Nasser's army, but they could not win world opinion. The United States opposed its three allies and joined with Russia to halt the fighting. Sadat watched the superpowers closely. At the height of the battle, Russia turned down Egypt's plea for aid. Sadat concluded it was a mistake ever to depend on the Soviets. But when Egypt asked President Dwight Eisenhower for help, he pressured his own allies to withdraw. They did, leaving Egypt in control of the canal. Sadat was impressed that Eisenhower had turned Egypt's military defeat into a political victory. He could not understand why Nasser praised Russia instead of the United States of America.

Egypt for Egyptians continued to be Nasser's goal. He nationalized banks, insurance companies, and businesses owned by Europeans to make up for the damage from British and French air raids.

At the height of the Suez crisis, Sadat's son was born. Although there were often weeks and sometimes months of tension between Sadat and Nasser, the Sadats chose the name Gamal for their son. A year later their second daughter, Noha, was born. In 1960 their family was complete with the birth of another daughter, Jihan, nicknamed Nana. The cost of supporting both his families worried Sadat. His oldest daughter, Rokaya, was married. He decided to close the

house of his first wife and bring his daughters Rawia, thirteen, and Camelia, ten, to live with him and Jihan. Both these girls missed their mother. Camelia also missed her joking, happy father. Now he appeared to her solemn, short-tempered, and preoccupied.

Sadat claimed that in the 1950s the revolution won colossal achievements, and in the 1960s made colossal mistakes. In 1958 Egypt and Syria had joined governments. That union, known as the United Arab Republic, was falling apart. Everything else seemed to be also. Nasser developed diabetes. Sadat was exhausted. In addition to his duties on the council, he was chairman of the Afro-Asian Solidarity Conference. He traveled to West Africa where the hot, humid air made him perspire uncomfortably. During the conference, Russia and China were at each other's throats over a treaty. Observers marveled at Sadat's endless patience as he negotiated a compromise. But the difficulty of those negotiations further tired him. When he returned to Cairo, conflict with Nasser continued. Suddenly on May 15, 1960, Sadat, at age forty-two, had a heart attack. Nasser came to the house while Sadat was recovering and smoothed over their differences.

Now Sadat had a new worry. What would happen to his families if he died. In Muslim countries girls often marry young to husbands chosen by their parents. Sadat decided that Rawia and Camelia should have husbands to provide for them. He chose army officers and arranged a double wedding on October 10, 1961. Rawia was fifteen; her husband thirty-two. Camelia was twelve and her husband twenty-nine.

Conditions in Egypt continued to worsen. Sadat urged the council to support the revolutionaries in Yemen, southeast of Egypt. Soon Egypt had seventy thousand soldiers there. This left little money for housing and farming projects in Egypt. Angry students staged demonstrations. Muslim fundamentalists tried a second time to assassinate Nasser, who retaliated by cracking down on all protesters. Egyptians were afraid to say a word, lest they be thrown in jail, lose their jobs and homes, and see their wives and children turned out on the street.

The Arab world looked to Nasser for leadership against Israel. They criticized him for permitting Israeli shipping to use the Tiran Strait at the entrance of the Gulf of Aqaba. This was Israel's only exit to the Red Sea and the right to use it had been guaranteed to Israel at the end of the 1956 war.

Nasser called the council together. He said, "If we close the Strait, war will be a one hundred percent certainty."[15] The council was confident about its military strength. Sadat voted with the others to close the strait. They also moved their troops to the Israeli border. Israel called Egypt's action an act of war. The council expected Israel to strike swiftly. All weekend Egyptian soldiers scanned the skies.

On Monday morning, June 5, 1967, Abdel Hakim Amer, Nasser's field marshal, decided to make an inspection tour of the Sinai. He ordered Egyptian anti-aircraft guns to hold their fire until he landed. Israel chose that moment to attack, beginning the Six-Day War. Egyptian planes sitting on the ground made easy targets.

"I was confident of victory," Sadat said. "I did not rush out and put on my clothes, but entered the bathroom to shave and take a shower as I did every morning. Then I told my driver to take me to army headquarters."[16] Amer stood there, his eyes aimlessly shifting back and forth. Sadat turned to the others. "What has happened?"[17]

"The Israelis have destroyed our entire air force,"[18] they answered.

"The news came as a thunderbolt. . . . I felt bitter as I fell on a couch . . . a million questions erupting inside me."[19]

That night air-raid sirens screamed over Cairo. "My youngest daughter, Nana, was six years old," Sadat said, "and was frightened every time she heard a gun or a rocket. I sent the children to the ground floor, then to Mit Abul-Kum, where I had built a home."[20]

While Sadat was in despair, Egyptians all around him were celebrating. The radio had been announcing great victories. How Sadat hated the deception. He suffered as much from the lies as the defeat. The truth was that by the end of the Six-Day War, Israelis had conquered the Gaza Strip, the

Sinai Peninsula, East Jerusalem, the West Bank of the Jordan River, and the Golan Heights in Syria.

At last Nasser spoke to the Egyptian people. "We cannot hide from ourselves the fact that we have met with a grave setback in the last few days,"[21] he said. But he blamed the defeat on the United States. Then he announced his resignation from "every official post and every political role."[22] Within minutes crowds were shrieking, "Don't leave us, Abdel Nasser."[23] The boss agreed to "bow to the voice of the people"[24] and keep his job.

Sadat remained loyal to Nasser during the next difficult years. They tried to restore Egypt's pride by rebuilding the armed forces and starting a war of attrition—a series of bombing and commando raids against Israeli forces in the Sinai. Each attack brought retaliation. Egypt sank an Israeli destroyer. Israel bombed an oil refinery. Egyptian forces ambushed Israeli patrols. Israel bombed a power station on the Nile. Soldiers and civilians died. Throughout this fighting, Nasser maintained, "What was taken away by force cannot be recovered except by force! We are committed to four principles: no recognition of Israel, no peace with Israel, no negotiation with Israel, and no interference in the Palestine issue."[25]

On December 19, 1969, Nasser announced that he was appointing Sadat vice-president. Sadat answered, "I don't want to be Vice-President. I shall carry on, and work side by side with you. If I must have a title, Presidental Advisor will be quite adequate."

"Oh, no!" Nasser said, "You must call tomorrow to be sworn in."[26]

Both men considered the problems Nasser's successor would face—Egypt's faltering economy and its disastrous military defeat. "Strangely enough," Sadat said, "I had been convinced for a long time that I was going to die before Nasser. Even more strangely, Nasser thought so as well and had promised to take care of my children after my death. This was after the heart attack I had about that time."[27] Nasser had one too. Still they carried on.

Nasser continued to emphasize the Arabness of Egypt. The country was called the United Arab Republic. School books did not even mention the name Egypt.

Nasser went to Russia asking for weapons to replace those lost in the Six-Day War. A "hopeless case" he told Sadat on his return. He used the English words, Sadat recalled, because none in Arabic could express his utter frustration. By the summer of 1970 Nasser said, "Listen, Anwar, whether we like it or not, all the cards of this game are in America's hands."[28] Nasser decided to accept a peace plan proposed by the United States Secretary of State William Rogers. The plan included a ninety-day cease-fire to give the United Nations time to work out a settlement.

As leader of the Arab world, Nasser tried to solve the problem of the Palestinian refugees. The king of Jordan had brutally attacked the Palestinians and forced them out of his country. Thousands were massacred. Nasser called an Arab conference. The strain of the difficult negotiations overwhelmed him. At the end of the meeting he was pale and perspiring. He couldn't even take a step.

Sadat's phone rang. By the time Sadat reached Nasser's bedside, Egypt's first president was dead. "I turned to the doctors and said: 'It's not true. . . . It can't be right!'"[29] Sadat was weeping when, on September 28, 1970, he announced on television, "The Arab nation and humanity have lost the most precious man."[30]

Chapter 5

YEAR OF DECISION; YEAR OF STAGNATION

Who was this Anwar el-Sadat? Leaders around the world all knew the name Nasser. Millions of Arabs idolized the strong man of Egypt. At his death, the country exploded with grief. But Sadat was a question mark. While other Free Officers scrambled for power, he had stayed on the sidelines, assisting Nasser. Behind his back, people called him "Major Yes Yes," or "Nasser's Poodle," he seemed so anxious to please.

United States diplomats who came to Nasser's funeral told President Richard Nixon that Sadat wouldn't stay in power more than a month or two. They underestimated the prisoner from cell 54.

At first Anwar el-Sadat thought he could govern as vice-president. But from the time of the pharaohs, Egyptians preferred a strong leader. The title "president" sounded powerful. Sadat decided to hold elections quickly.

That news disturbed three important members of the government led by Ali Sabri. They considered themselves better qualified to continue Nasser's policies. All three approved Nasser's close ties with Russia and feared Sadat would try to patch up Egypt's relationship with the United

States. They intended to push aside "Nasser's Poodle" and take control of the Egyptian government themselves.

Sadat was nominated for president. Egyptians voted *naam* (yes) or *la* (no). On October 15, 1970, 90.04 percent voted yes. Two days later, at age fifty-two, Sadat was inaugurated. Would the Ali Sabri group let him stay in power?

Once in charge, Sadat acted to change the atmosphere of despair and fear that gripped the country. Nasser had turned Egypt into a police state. "What is this?"[1] Sadat asked when given a stack of papers.

"The text of tapped telephone conversations between certain people being watched,"[2] Nasser's advisor replied.

Sadat was appalled. Hundreds of private telephones had been tapped on Nasser's orders. Furiously Sadat pushed the papers away. "I don't like to read such rubbish. . . . I'll have nothing to do with it."[3] Henceforth, phone tapping required a court order. "Fear is, I believe, a most effective tool in destroying the soul of an individual—and the soul of a people,"[4] Sadat said.

When Sadat took office he promised to make 1971 a Year of Decision. In January he addressed his first mass rally about regaining the Sinai. "There will be no compromise," he said, "and we will not give up one inch of our land. The battle will extend to our farms, our factories, in the towns, cities, and on the streets. Are you *really* fed up? Are you *really* tired of fighting?" he demanded. The crowd roared,

"We shall fight! O Sadat, lead us to liberation."[5]

They wanted liberation of the Sinai, which Israel had conquered in the Six-Day War. Sadat put the world on notice. In this Year of Decision 1971, he intended to get the Sinai back—either by negotiation or war. Meanwhile he extended the Rogers Plan ninety-day cease-fire. He needed time to think.

"My brother is slow in making decisions," Sadat's sister, Sekina, said. "He has learned to think everything over very carefully, even the smallest decisions concerning his children."[6]

Sadat analyzed the Arab-Israeli conflict. Since 1948 the Arabs' goal had been to destroy Israel and push it into the sea. Arab countries would not recognize Israel's right to exist or talk with Israel face-to-face. After the Six-Day War, in 1967, the Arabs' immediate goal was to recover the lost territory. Some Arab countries were willing to consider accepting Israel's existence. Israel refused to give up the occupied territories until the Arabs promised peace and secure borders. Israel pointed out that at one place its country was only eight miles wide, between the occupied West Bank and the Mediterranean Sea.

The Arabs' position was first return the territory, then we'll talk about recognition. The Israelis' position was first grant recognition, then we'll talk about returning the territory.

President Sadat concluded that Egypt was not strong enough to destroy Israel. Any attempt would lead to another defeat and more enormous war debts. Therefore he had to win back the Sinai through negotiation.

On February 4, 1971, Sadat announced an entirely new initiative. If Israel pulled back halfway across the Sinai, Egypt would sign a peace agreement with Israel, negotiated by a United Nations representative.

In Arabic there are two words for peace. *Sulkh* is a peace of forgiveness and acceptance. *Saalam* means a state of no war. Israel wanted *sulkh*. Sadat was offering *saalam*. The Israelis rejected the initiative because it did not offer the two things Israel wanted most: recognition of its existence and face-to-face talks with Egypt. Until Sadat offered these, Israel wanted to keep the rugged Sinai desert as a buffer zone between enemies. In addition, the Israelis were not sure Sadat could be trusted. The United States was also cool to Sadat's initiative.

Sadat was planning a family celebration. In the middle of the night of May 11, 1971, a policeman rang the Sadats' doorbell and insisted on personally delivering two tape recordings to the president. Sadat was stunned to hear men from the opposition Ali Sabri group planning his assassination. According to the tapes he had just a few hours to live.

Jihan Sadat recalled, "We didn't sleep that night. . . . My husband always sleeps with a pistol beside his bed. . . . That night I wanted to lock the bedroom door, and told him 'This way, if they come, you will be ready with your pistol.' . . . I went upstairs to my oldest daughter, Lubna, and suggested she sleep that night in the house of my sister. She was only seventeen, but she said, 'If they blow up the house, do you think we would be happy living without our father and mother?' She took her book and went upstairs to bed. My son Gamal was only fifteen, but he got his small bird gun and insisted on being bodyguard. 'I want to protect my father,' he said."[7]

"What was really painful," Sadat later admitted, "was the discovery that my own house had been bugged."[8]

Sadat moved quickly. First he made certain that the army was loyal. Then he dismissed the leader of the plotters. The other conspirators resigned their positions in protest. They expected to cripple the government and expose Sadat's weakness, but their scheme backfired. Sadat accepted their resignations and then arrested them. But he didn't stop there. Soon he had arrested or dismissed hundreds of government employees and army officers loyal to the conspirators.

Jokes about "Major Yes Yes" ended. Portraits of Sadat sprang up replacing Nasser's pictures that had continued to hang everywhere. Newspapers talked about the "May 15 revolution." Sadat wasn't temporary anymore. He gave back to the Egyptian people what he considered their most precious possession—freedom. "I called on everybody to do and say what he liked, as long as he broke no laws,"[9] Sadat said.

As president, Sadat's life changed on the outside. Green lawns and palm-lined walkways surrounded his official residence, the Barrages, on the east coast of the Nile. King Farouk's Abdin Palace now served as his office. Jihan filled their Cairo home with French furniture. Sadat had always loved fine clothes, though often he had owned only one shabby suit. Now he indulged his fancy with smartly tailored outfits and pure silk ties.

But the man inside those elegant trappings was still the villager from Mit Abul-Kum. He never smoked his pipe or even crossed his feet in front of his father. That would have shown disrespect. Despite being an army officer, he did not give orders. He preferred to say please. And when he said thank you, he added "my son" to the office boy or the attendant who brought him tea.

His taste in food, unlike his taste in clothes, was very simple. Breakfast was a spoonful of honey, and lunch a bowl of soup. The years in cell 54 had left him with a tender stomach. He avoided rich food in favor of boiled vegetables, fruit, minted tea, and juice. As a devout Muslim, he never touched wine or liquor.

Nasser had signed letters until 3:00 A.M. the day he died of a heart attack. Sadat was not a workaholic president. Jihan rose at five, but Anwar slept until nine and often napped in the afternoon. He took a good quick walk every day because he considered it necessary to train the body as well as the mind.

Despite his leisurely schedule, Sadat completed his presidential duties. In his view, a president was a decision maker. He left paperwork to his ministers. One aide said, "Our main job is to protect the boss from details."[10] Reading reports was one detail Sadat hated. Assistants read them and gave him short oral summaries.

Sadat turned his attention to the Russians—his arms suppliers. Israel's army bristled with the latest American weapons of war. Make Egypt equal, Sadat begged the Soviets. In the past the U.S.S.R. had promised equipment, then not delivered it, or delivered less advanced models. Exasperated, Sadat complained, "You cannot imagine what my life has been like since I became President. There has hardly been a quiet day without some quarrel with the Russians. They never trusted me. . . . My tongue went dry arguing with them."[11]

Sadat went to Russia in March 1971. If his peace efforts failed, he would need weapons for war. Israel had American Phantom jets. Sadat asked the Russians for MIG 25s. The Soviets claimed Egyptian pilots would need five years to master the complicated jets. They agreed to supply them, but insisted the planes have Russian pilots and remain under Russian command. Sadat flatly refused.

Later Sadat agreed to take the planes with Russian pilots until his own were trained. There were already thousands of Russian advisors and technicians in Egypt working on the Aswan High Dam and military installations. Their numbers had grown steadily under Nasser.

The MIGs did not arrive, but the president of Russia did. He had a treaty of friendship, which he insisted Egypt sign immediately. He gave his word that the planes would arrive within four days. Four months later, nothing had been shipped.

Sadat's next visit to Russia in October ended with more unfulfilled promises. He was at his wits' end. The Year of Decision was running out. Angry university students staged a rally accusing Sadat of empty words and demanding war against Israel. Police used tear gas to stop their march on Cairo. Sadat was shaken by these demonstrations. They threatened his presidency. So did nearly a million refugees from the bombed-out Suez Canal cities who waited in make-shift camps. They were tired of Sadat's endless promises. They wanted action to remove Israeli guns from the Sinai so they could return to their homes. Sadat put on a khaki uniform to visit the troops at the Suez Canal. "I have come to tell you," he said, "that the time to fight has come, that there is no more hope. Our next meeting will be in Sinai."[12]

After Sadat made more visits to Russia, the Soviets promised to ship the needed weapons by November 1972, election month in the United States. Sadat had one last hope for a peaceful solution, but he needed America's help. He wanted the newly-elected American president to produce a workable peace plan. If the United States failed, Sadat said, "We are going to war."

In May 1972 President Nixon visited Russia. He and Soviet Secretary General Leonid Brezhnev agreed to cut down tension in the Middle East. Sadat was still waiting for his promised planes when the Soviet ambassador gave him a letter. It talked about friendship, but did not say a word about weapons. That was the last straw.

"Well," Sadat said, "Please convey . . . an official message. . . . I have decided to dispense with the services of all Soviet military experts [about fifteen thousand] . . . they must go back to the Soviet Union within one week from today."[13] The ambassador was aghast. Sadat was ordering the Russians out of Egypt. In five minutes he had broken a seventeen-year relationship.

Americans were delighted to see the Russians lose influence in the Middle East. Across the Sinai, many Israeli leaders concluded that Sadat had given up the idea of war.

Sadat's shock tactics of expelling the Russians worked. "They are drowning me in new arms,"[14] Sadat reported. Between December 1972 and June 1973 Russian missiles, tanks, and bridging equipment poured into Egypt. "It looks as if they want to push me into battle,"[15] he said. Sadat hoped American policy would change too and that the United States would offer the economic aid Egypt needed so desperately.

Since 1967 Egypt had been prepared for war with Israel. Year after year the huge Egyptian army was "sitting on the Canal trapping sandflies,"[16] as it waited for battles that never came. There was no war; there was no peace; and there was no longer any money.

"When I took over power," Sadat wrote, "I realized the bitter truth. . . . [The] Minister of Finance . . . said simply that the treasury was empty and we were 'almost bankrupt.'. . . I was very perturbed to learn that . . . we might soon find it difficult to pay the salaries of our soldiers on the front and the salaries of civil servants. . . . [If] they couldn't be paid—if they came to know that their families back home had no food to eat—wouldn't they desert the front? Wouldn't Egypt collapse?"[17]

The cost of the Aswan Dam and the war in Yemen added to the problem. So had Nasser's economic policy of nationalizing most private businesses. People did not work as hard for the government as they had for themselves.

Time and money were running out for Sadat. Other Arab nations pressured Sadat to take action to erase the 1967 losses. Finally he said, "The basic task was to wipe out the disgrace and humiliation that followed from the 1967 defeat. I reckoned it would be 1,000 times more honorable for us—

40,000 of my sons in the armed forces and myself—to be buried crossing the canal, than to accept such disgrace and humiliation. Posterity would say we had died honorably on the battlefield."[18]

Egyptian soldiers occupy an Israeli defense line in Sinai (October 1973).

Chapter 6

THE $\left\{\begin{array}{l}\text{OCTOBER} \\ \text{YOM KIPPUR} \\ \text{RAMADAN}\end{array}\right\}$ WAR

The date October 6, 1973, 10 Tishrel 5734, 10 Ramadan 1393, turned out to be an important one on all three calendars—Western, Jewish, and Muslim. The fourth Arab-Israeli war started on that day. Sadat had begun preparing for the war many months before.

As he paced back and forth along the path at his summer home in Alexandria or his house near the pyramids, he analyzed past wars. He blamed Egyptian defeats on poor leadership, and Israeli victories on surprise. Surprise was a powerful weapon. Sadat intended to keep his war plans secret from everyone, especially Americans, Russians, and Israelis. But he never expected to keep them secret from his own generals. Yet when the Supreme Council of the Armed Forces met, he was flabbergasted to discover that some of his generals knew nothing.

"May I inquire what exactly was that 'message' that you sent us?" one major-general asked Sadat, referring to an order to prepare for war that he should have received in the summer. "I had no idea that any message had been sent by Your Excellency."

"What's the meaning of this?" Sadat demanded of his war minister.

The war minister whispered, "I thought it unadvisable, sir, to tell everybody. So I just informed the commanders of the armies, so as to maintain secrecy."

"Should a war decision be kept from the very people who are going to fight?"[1] Sadat wondered.

Sadat faced more unpleasant discoveries. Egyptian forces on the west bank of the Suez Canal lay directly open to the Israelis, who were dug in behind huge earthworks of sand on the canal's east bank. Originally both sides had played a deadly game of one-upmanship with their fortifications. Each time the Israelis heaped on three feet of sand, the Egyptians added five. But Egypt's war minister had called a halt. Now the Israeli fortifications towered forty-seven feet in the air. Sadat changed war ministers and ordered his fortifications raised to sixty-five feet.

Although preparations for war continued, Sadat sent his advisor to Washington, D.C. to meet with National Security Advisor Henry Kissinger. War could still be avoided if the United States worked out an acceptable peace plan. When Sadat did not get American support, he turned to his Arab and African friends. The Organization of African Unity was holding a summit conference. Sadat convinced the members there to pass a resolution condemning Israel.

Oil, Sadat knew, could be a more destructive weapon than

missiles. Europe, Japan, and the United States depended on Arab oil to fuel their factories. Sadat asked King Feisal of Saudi Arabia, the biggest oil producer in the Middle East, to use its oil to help Egypt. Saudi Arabia warned the world that countries not siding with the Arabs against Israel would lose their "liquid gold."

Sadat continued working to win allies to his side. Finally he said, "Three weeks before Zero Hour the support of more than a hundred countries had been secured. It had taken me many months—from January to September—to prepare the world for the war."[2]

Syria's partnership was crucial to Sadat's battle plan. Syria and Jordan, Israel's neighbors, also had lost territory in the Six-Day War. "I'll be with you," Syria's president, Hafez al-Assad, had told Sadat in April 1973. "We're going to fight and are preparing for it."[3]

Now they had to decide when the battle would begin. Tides in the canal were best for crossing in May, August-September, and October of 1973. Sadat chose the October date because October 6 was Yom Kippur, the holiest day in the Jewish year. Jews fasted and prayed in synagogues throughout that day of repentance. The Israeli nation practically shut down. Television, radio, and transportation services closed.

Muslims would be observing the month-long fast of Ramadan during which they do not eat or drink from sunup to sundown. However, an Islamic expert advised Sadat that those involved in the war were exempt from fasting.

Then, to throw Israel off the track, Sadat launched a campaign of misinformation. First he staged army maneuvers to convince Israel that an attack was coming in May. The strategy worked. Israel called up its troops at a cost of ten million dollars. Sadat repeated the procedure in August. Again Israel went on full alert. By the time the real attack came in October, Israel had ignored Egypt's third military buildup as yet another fake, refusing to be "tricked" into one more useless ten-million-dollar mobilization.

Next Sadat had false stories placed in newspapers about army officers going on pilgrimages. Soldiers were encouraged to swim in the canal as if on vacation. Sadat made a point of revealing to visiting Western diplomats that he believed the Arabs could not possibly win a war against Israel. He knew they would pass the news on to Israelis who would assume no attack was planned.

Sadat also wanted to rally people's sympathy. Egypt did not want to look like the aggressor by starting the war. It was decided to accuse Israel of breaking the cease-fire by raiding an Egyptian post called Zafarana on the Red Sea. This false story was broadcast on the radio and followed by a second report that Egypt was sending soldiers to put down the attack with force.

Throughout this time, Sadat made inspection tours of

army units. He wanted to see for himself that they were ready for combat. He ordered them to practice the actual tasks that they would perform at the invasion. They used the Nile irrigation canals. "We trained for this mission for a long time," one Egyptian soldier said. "Each of us knew by heart what he was supposed to do."[4] Sadat also prepared the home front. Factories and power stations all had battle plans.

These war preparations were costing Egypt money that it didn't have. On September 30, Sadat announced that Egypt's economy had fallen below zero. The country could not repay its bank loans. "In three months' time . . . we shan't have enough bread in the pantry!"[5] he said. The minister of supply had more bad news. He said there wasn't enough food for a long war.

Sadat worried about his own family. After becoming president he had kept a formal distance between himself and the three daughters from his first marriage. They were told to ask permission before coming to visit. Now Sadat asked Rawia and Camelia to come to Mit Abul-Kum. "'Do you have groceries?' he asked. . . . 'sugar, tea, oil . . . things like that? I want you to build up your supplies of food.'"[6] Since they knew nothing about the coming war, they were surprised by their father's questions and his preoccupation with their food supplies.

By October 3, Sadat decided it was time to tell Russia that Syria and Egypt intended to end the Middle East stalemate—by war. "What will the Soviet attitude be?"[7] he asked their ambassador. Sadat did not get the reaction he wanted. Instead of offering support, the Soviets asked permission to land four giant transport planes. They planned to fly all Russian families out of Egypt. Apparently Russia expected the Arab forces to lose the war. The Soviets ordered their supply ship, which was due to dock in Egypt with more weapons, "to wander around a little in the Mediterranean"[8] instead. They did not want these new armaments destroyed in the fighting.

"On Friday, [October 5] I went . . . to the modest little mosque where I had learned to pray fifty years before. . . . My peace of mind was perfect," Sadat said. "Though conscious of the decisiveness of the moments to come, I looked forward to tomorrow when war would rock the world. . . . I approached the battle without the least agitation or nervousness."[9]

The secrecy of the war plans extended to Jihan. Sadat did not discuss presidential matters with his family. Very often they learned about his actions at the same time as other Egyptians from the radio and television. Jihan suspected war was coming but did not know when. "I asked him [Sadat] if I should keep the children home from school the next day. He said, 'No, send them along, like the others.' I said that at least I would keep our car in front of the school, just in case. He agreed, but advised me not to bother till noon. I knew then that the war would break out around midday."[10]

At 2:00 P.M. October 6, with Israel observing Yom Kippur prayers and the sun directly in the eyes of the Israeli soldiers manning the Sinai defenses, Egypt sent 222 supersonic jets streaking across the Suez Canal. Three thousand guns burst into action. The effect of this thunderous attack stunned the Israelis, the world, and even the Egyptians. "It surprised us . . . by achieving 90 percent of its targets,"[11] claimed Sadat. One of the planes that did not return had been piloted by Atif, Sadat's youngest brother. His death devastated Sadat, who had raised Atif and considered him a son.

Egyptian soldiers shouting *"Allahu Akbar!"* ("Allah is greater") boarded boats to cross the canal. The forty-seven-foot walls of sand that the Israelis had erected presented a major obstacle, but the Egyptians were prepared. They had ordered extra-powerful high-pressure water pumps from Germany, supposedly for fire department use. Jet streams of water cut through the sand like a sword through butter. Soon there were gaping holes in the walls, large enough for tanks to rumble through. By nightfall the Egyptians had accomplished what many military experts around the world considered impossible. They had crossed the canal, stormed the barricades, and put Israel's fortifications out of commission.

"I used to tell Nasser," Sadat said, "that if we could recapture even 4 inches of Sinai territory . . . then the whole situation would change. . . . First to go would be the humiliation we had endured since the 1967 defeat; for to cross into Sinai and hold on to any territory recaptured would restore our self-confidence."[12] Now that the crossing was complete, Sadat announced, "No matter what happens in the desert, there has been a victory that cannot be erased."[13] An Arab writer said, "What matters is that the world now no longer will laugh at us when we threaten to fight. . . . It will have to take us seriously."[14] Arabs everywhere exulted that their pride had been restored. "Even if we lose the war," one said, "we have won."[15]

The north was also a scene of battle as the Syrians launched their own attack at 2:00 P.M. The Syrians drove hard against the Israelis who exchanged prayer shawls for machine guns as they rushed to defend their borders.

Within six hours of the first artillery blast, the Russian ambassador came to see Sadat. He claimed that Syria had asked him to request a cease-fire within forty-eight hours. President Sadat was shocked. Was the Russian speaking the truth? Why hadn't President Assad mentioned this directly? As soon as the ambassador left, Sadat sent a coded message to Assad, who denied making the request. The one clear fact in this murky situation was that the Russians wanted a cease-fire at all costs. They still feared Egypt and Syria would lose the war. United States Secretary of State Henry Kissinger was also working on a cease-fire. He called the foreign ministers of Egypt and Israel, but his pleas to halt the fighting failed.

The next night, October 7, Egyptian forces were still pushing ahead. The Soviet ambassador came again to present Syria's second request for a cease-fire. When Sadat told him of Syria's denial, the Russian turned white. "Now listen," Sadat said, "this subject is closed; . . . I won't have a cease-fire until the objectives of the battle have been achieved. I'd like you to tell the Moscow leadership to send me some tanks at once. This will be the biggest tank battle in history."[16]

If not the biggest, it was perhaps the most desperate as shown by the horrifying destruction of life, machinery, and morale. The bodies of fallen soldiers dotted the sand. After three days of fighting, both sides saw their traveling steel fortresses reduced to burned-out hulks. Syria lost twelve hundred tanks in one day.

Both sides begged the superpowers to rearm them. Soviet transports carrying ammunition and equipment landed at Syrian and Egyptian airports on October 9 and 10. The first of many United States supply planes flew to Israel on October 14. Sadat quickly discovered who his friends were. "We were in great need of replacements. I found none but Tito [president of Yugoslavia] to ask for help. We asked for

100 tanks. . . . Tito, without delay, sent us 140 tanks, ready for immediate action. All were supplied with ammunition and their fuel tanks were filled up. . . . The tanks were transported directly by train to the front."[17]

Colonel Muammar Qaddafi (leader of Libya) "never did carry out his promises," said Sadat. "We sent tankers that he had promised would be returned to us filled with oil. . . . Much to our surprise, the tankers returned as empty as they had left."[18] Sadat turned to the Shah of Iran. The shah cabled, "On the way to you now are 600 tons of oil which were being shipped to Europe."[19] Other Arab nations including Jordan, Saudi Arabia, and Iraq sent men and matériel. North Korea and North Vietnam sent pilots and advisors to Egypt.

While the war dragged on, Jihan spent her days visiting hospitals and comforting the wounded. She helped roll bandages for the Egyptian Red Crescent (Red Cross) Society.

By October 10 the fortunes of Israel and Egypt were changing. The Israelis planned a daring crossing from the Sinai to the west bank of the canal. They intended to cross at Deversoir where they had discovered a weak spot in the Egyptian lines.

Sadat decided to address Egypt's National Assembly and present his plan for peace. As he drove to the parliament building, thousands lined the strets wildly cheering "Victory for Sadat!" From Cairo Sadat addressed the world through television and radio coverage. "We are fighting for the sake of peace," he said. "I would like to add, so they may hear in Israel: we are not advocates of annihilation." Sadat wanted to assure the Israelis that Egypt no longer wanted to destroy their state. "We are prepared to accept a cease-fire on condition that the Israeli forces withdraw forthwith from all occupied territories. . . . We are ready, once the withdrawal . . . has been carried out, to attend an international peace conference at the U.N. . . . [and] to start clearing the Suez Canal and open it to navigation."[20]

Israel's prime minister Golda Meir had also scheduled a speech at noon on Tuesday, October 16. She postponed hers to listen to Sadat. Then she announced that Israeli forces were fighting on both sides of the canal. If they were on the west bank, it was possible for them to battle their way toward Cairo, the heart of Egypt. Egypt's Third Army was dug in east of the canal. Once the Israelis had crossed to the west bank, they were able to come at this Third Army from both sides and surround it.

Sadat encountered more problems. He claimed the United States provided Israel with battle information. He said, "While the U.S. satellite hourly transmitted information to Israel, we received nothing at all from the Soviet satellite."[21] He also accused the United States of equipping Israel with new deadly rockets that were demolishing Egyptian missiles. "I knew my capabilities," Sadat said. "I did not intend to fight the entire United States of America."[22]

Before the war started, Sadat told Jihan, "I know I am doing my duty. I know I will win."[23] Each decision he made determined the fate of millions of Egyptians. Now he faced the difficult decision of whether or not to continue fighting. He said, "I would not allow the Egyptian forces . . . to be destroyed once again. And I was willing to be brought to book by my people in Egypt and the Arab world, to answer for this decision."[24]

On October 19, Sadat cabled Syrian president Assad that he was ready to accept a cease-fire. Then he ordered his generals to stop the Israelis from advancing to the west bank of the canal. These generals disagreed on whether this Israeli advance was dangerous. One who thought it was extremely serious, wanted help from the Egyptian forces fighting east of the canal in the Sinai desert. But to Sadat, those soldiers on the east bank represented Egypt's victory: her red, white, and black flag was flying over the Sinai once again. If he withdrew those troops by pulling them back across the canal, Sadat was afraid that the world would regard it as a sign of defeat. He told the generals "there was nothing to worry about. Consequently I issued an order, which I believe was even more important than that of the fighting order of October 6, that there should be no withdrawal at all (not a soldier, not a rifle, nothing) from the East Bank of the Canal to the West."[25]

Meanwhile, the battlefield of the October War widened to include roadside gasoline stations and factories across the United States, Europe, and Japan. Arab nations cut their oil production. They threatened to stop all shipments to the United States if the government didn't change its pro-Israel policy. As "No Gas" signs popped up around the world, the Arabs realized the effect of the oil weapon.

When Sadat said he was ready to accept a cease-fire, Kissinger went to Moscow to make the arrangements. On October 22, sixteen days after Sadat ordered his historic crossing into Sinai, the United Nations Security Council declared a cease-fire. During the three days that it took to negotiate the cease-fire, Israeli and Egyptian tanks, missiles, and men battled it out at Deversoir. Both sides suffered heavy casualties. By the 22nd, Israel claimed it had ten thousand men on the west bank and had cut the supply line to Egypt's Third Army.

The guns were scheduled to stop at 6:55 P.M. on October 22. They did not. Each side blamed the other for violating the cease-fire. Israel accused the Third Army of fighting to break out of its trap. Sadat claimed that the Third Army was not surrounded, and that Israeli units kept fighting in order to encircle it. In a fury, he contacted the superpowers. "Please come in," he said, "I am willing to have your forces land on Egyptian territory to ensure that the Israelis pull back to October 22 lines."[26]

That request scared nearly everyone. Did Sadat realize how dangerous it was to invite Soviet and American troops to the Middle East? Russia quickly agreed to send soldiers to enforce the cease-fire. To keep the Russians out, the United States ordered a worldwide nuclear alert. These threats worked. Soon there was silence along the fighting lines. But Sadat was demanding immediate action to free his Third Army.

The fourth Egyptian-Israeli war was now a standoff. Both sides could claim victory—Egypt in the first week, Israel in the second. Egypt had accomplished its goal of crossing the Suez Canal and defeating Israeli forces. It had destroyed the myth that Israel's air force and soldiers were superior. Israel had recovered from its initial losses, crossed the canal, and taken Egyptian territory to the west.

The fate of the Third Army could change everything. Israelis, still angered by the Yom Kippur attack and the early defeats, wanted an overwhelming victory. Israel could wipe out Egypt's accomplishments if it forced the Third Army to surrender by keeping its supply lines cut. The United States and Russia both wanted to save the Third Army. The Soviets had provided Egypt's weapons. If the army surrendered, it would imply Russian weapons were inferior. Henry Kissinger wanted to negotiate a peace agreement in the Middle East. To do so Egypt and Israel had to meet at the bargaining table as equals. There would be no

THE MIDDLE EAST IN 1974

☐ Occupied by Israel

▨ Israeli Withdrawals

LEBANON
Golan Heights
Quineitra
Haifa
SYRIA
MEDITERRANEAN SEA
Tel Aviv
West Bank
JORDAN R.
Amman
Port Said
Gaza
Jerusalem
DEAD SEA
Beersheba
El Arish
ISRAEL
SUEZ CANAL
Negev Desert
JORDAN
Cairo
Suez
Sinai Peninsula
Elat
Aqaba
NILE RIVER
EGYPT
GULF OF SUEZ
GULF OF AQABA
SAUDI ARABIA
Sharm el Sheik
STR. OF TIRAN
RED SEA

equality if the Third Army surrendered.

On October 29, Israel agreed to permit food, water, and medical supplies through its lines to the Third Army. Kissinger flew to Cairo and met with Sadat. "What are your requests?" he asked. "I want a return to the cease-fire lines of October 22,"[27] Sadat replied. The men talked for three hours. They finally agreed that Egypt and Israel would hold talks under United Nations auspices. They would discuss disengaging forces and returning to the October 22 cease-fire line. The talks would take place at kilometer 105 on the Cairo-Suez road.

93

The Egyptian destroyer *October 6*, with President Sadat aboard, enters the Suez Canal at Port Said on its reopening (June 1975).

Chapter 7

THE OPENING

At 3:00 P.M. on Monday, October 29, 1973, a helicopter carrying Israeli's chief negotiator landed at the tents set up for the talks. The Egyptians were nowhere in sight. Minutes ticked by—fifteen, thirty, forty-five, sixty. Meanwhile, the Egyptians called the United States State Department to ask why the Israelis had not shown up. Telephone calls flashed between Cairo and Washington; Washington and Tel Aviv. Tension, already sky-high, increased as both sides thought the worst of each other. Finally the crisis was solved. The Egyptians were waiting at kilometer 105. Israeli army units had put the tents at kilometer 101. The Israelis claimed that haste caused a mistake in measuring. The Egyptians claimed Israel wanted to delay the talks until the plight of the Third Army worsened. The two countries seemed unable to agree on anything.

The talks started the next day. They were a first for both nations. Previously, Arab countries had refused to speak directly to Israeli representatives. The United Nations or some authorized person acted as a go-between. Kissinger, who had acted as intermediary, said Egypt never would agree to direct talks. Kissinger underestimated Anwar el-

Sadat. He underestimated Sadat's willingness to break with the past when the past no longer served his goals. At kilometer 101 the United Nations supervised the talks, but Sadat permitted his representative to negotiate directly with Israel's spokesman. Later a photograph of the two generals, Major General Aharon Yariv from Israel and Lieutenant General Abdel Ghany el-Gamasy from Egypt, shaking hands caused trouble for Sadat with many Arabs.

Inside the tent at kilometer 101, the Egyptian and Israeli objectives kept them dangerously far apart. Like two men in a high-stakes card game, both negotiators had a set of cards to play. Egypt's high card was the Israeli prisoners of war. Israeli citizens were putting tremendous pressure on their government to get these men back. Israel's high card was its blockade of Egypt's Third Army.

Egypt had demanded that Israel return to the October 22 cease-fire line, which would free the Third Army. Israel wanted its prisoners returned before any pullback occurred. Neither side would budge one inch. The talks were getting nowhere.

Sadat had a philosophy for solving problems. "Approaching a given problem, I do all in my power to provide a radical and final solution rather than a temporary one."[1] Sadat's ultimate goal was a peace agreement. He did not want the talks to break down over returning to the October 22 cease-fire line—a temporary solution to protect his army.

Sadat agreed to exchange prisoners of war without Israel's return to the October 22 battle lines. Sadat's foreign minister was shocked. He insisted Sadat had played his best card and gotten nothing in return. By November 10, Egypt and Israel signed an agreement to work for a permanent separation of forces under United Nations supervision. Twelve days later, 241 Israeli and 8,031 Egyptian prisoners had been exchanged.

Jihan received a letter from an Israeli mother whose son had been killed in Egypt. She begged Mrs. Sadat to help locate his body. (Jihan asked the minister of defense to search, but the body was never found.) "All my friends . . . said I could not write to the enemy," Jihan said. But she did reply to the letter without asking her husband for permission. "My husband scolded me for contacting Israelis. He said it was too early."[2]

A month after the prisoner exchange, Sadat said, "At this point I was in great pain. I was suffering daily, hourly. I could see no way out—everything seemed to have gone wrong, and I wasn't able to put it right because it was no longer up to me. . . . The doctors who examined me . . . said it was due to tension but that it wasn't really serious."[3]

Sadat's tension resulted from the fact that Israeli troops were occupying Egyptian soil at Deversoir. The talks at kilometer 101 had broken down. Sadat ended them. "I am not prepared to engage in this sort of haggling and bickering,"[4] he announced. Sadat wanted all Israeli troops out of Egyptian territory. He did not want to argue about it inch by inch. But the Israelis did not trust the man who, despite his peace initiative, had ordered a surprise attack against them. As one soldier said, "We are giving up territory, and all the Arabs are giving up is their signature on a piece of paper. They signed a piece of paper in 1949—and we have had to fight three wars since then."[5]

"I am going to liquidate the Israeli Deversoir pocket,"[6] Sadat announced to Kissinger, and asked what the American attitude would be. Sadat said Kissinger warned him that the United States would strike at Egypt. Kissinger begged Sadat to go to Geneva, Switzerland for peace talks at the end of December. Sadat liked Henry Kissinger. He said, "For the first time, I felt as if I was looking at the real face of the United States, the one I had always wanted to see."[7] He agreed to go to Geneva.

The December chill of Switzerland penetrated the conference room. Although Arab and Israeli delegations sat in the same room, they entered by separate doors and refused to sit next to each other. The conference was delayed forty-five minutes while seats were rearranged. With that frigid atmosphere, the representatives decided to keep the conference short. The main accomplishment was an agreement between Israel and Egypt to hold more talks in January 1974.

Henry Kissinger increased his peacemaking efforts in a style that came to be known as "shuttle diplomacy." Like the shuttle of a weaving loom that flies back and forth pulling the thread, Henry Kissinger flew from Cairo to Tel Aviv and back again. When Sadat caught bronchitis and went to Aswan, Kissinger flew there too. He hammered out a compromise by which enemy troops at Deversoir were finally separated. It was agreed that Israeli troops would leave the west bank of the canal and pull back fourteen miles from the east bank. In return, Sadat promised to reopen the canal and let supplies pass through it to Israel—although not in Israeli ships. He also promised to rebuild the canal cities that had been abandoned since the bombings of the Six-Day War. These new cities would be Sadat's hostages—to peace.

Sadat turned his attention from the drab tents at kilometer 101 to a grand tent pitched on the bank of the Nile. His daughter, Lubna, was celebrating her marriage. The previous fall he had told her that they would have to postpone the celebration until after the wartime state of emergency. Now with a troop separation agreement signed, the Sadats and their guests dined on roast duck, sea bass, and a wedding cake six feet high. Among the guests, Sadat included a group of wounded soldiers who came in their hospital pajamas. The bridal couple were escorted into the tent behind twelve belly dancers as a forty-five-piece Arab orchestra played.

The crossing that Sadat ordered on October 6 changed Egypt's national mood. One poet who had criticized Sadat now wrote:

> I had never before believed in the role of the individual in history.
> I did not know that one person alone, in setting his own will, set that of a Nation, and the history of a people, and the strength of a civilization.
> But the hero, Anwar el-Sadat, is beyond my ken.
> He crushed the defeat lying deep within us all when he resolved upon the crossing.
> And by his decision not only the army crossed the Canal
> But the people crossed with it and transcended their submissiveness and misery, left behind their humiliation and shame . . .
> The crossing is deliverance.[8]

Sadat was the hero who had restored Egypt's pride. Egyptians no longer felt inferior to the Israelis. Their uplifted mood spread far beyond the Nile. All Arab nations shared in this renewed sense of dignity. Shrewdly, Sadat recognized that his new hero status gave him much more power. An Egyptian commander had said, "When you are victorious, you can afford to be generous and noble."[9] Sadat might have added ". . . and take risks."

Predictably, the second round of disengagement talks broke down. Israeli guns still pointed at the canal. Nonetheless Sadat said, "I want to rebuild those towns right within range of Israeli guns. I want to show the Israelis that I don't intend to make war against them again."[10]

If the decision to clear the canal was difficult, actually clearing it was almost impossible. The Suez Canal was one gigantic mine field. Not hundreds, not thousands, but hundreds of thousands of land mines, antitank mines, and bombs blocked the waterway. Barges, boats, trucks, tanks, airplanes, oil drums, and bridge sections clogged its path. The cost of clearing and dredging might exceed a billion dollars. Where could Sadat find the money or the equipment? He turned to Henry Kissinger.

"Am I to understand that you're asking for assistance?" Kissinger said.

"Yes," Sadat replied.

"Well, give me an hour."[11] Kissinger called the White House and the Pentagon. When he returned, he announced that a United States ship with the necessary equipment would be steaming toward the canal the next day. Helicopters with minesweeping sleds would follow. Other nations also made loans of money and machinery.

In the morning haze of June 5, 1975, Sadat's car drove

slowly toward the canal. Girls blew kisses, and men beat the air with their fists while chanting, 'Ya Sadat, ya Sadat."[12] Suddenly an aged, thin man with white hair down to his shoulders stepped forward. As guards rushed to remove him, Sadat asked his driver to stop. The man stared at Sadat for a moment, then kneeled in prayer. For Sadat, that old man symbolized the joy of the 700,000 Egyptians who could now return to the homes and cities they had fled eight years before. Sadat, dressed in a white admiral's uniform, rode down the canal on the deck of a destroyer called *October Six*. "This is one of the happiest moments of my life," he said. Along the banks banners displayed the message, "WE HAVE OPENED THE CANAL. WE WILL KEEP IT OPEN."[13]

Now that Sadat had opened the canal, he wanted to open Egypt to foreign investors. "Egypt's future depends on industrialization,"[14] he said. That required vast sums of money. Under Nasser, foreign investors had left Egypt after their private industries and businesses had been taken over by the state. Sadat issued the October Working Paper, which was a plan to win Western and Arab dollars to the Nile. His program protected foreign investors from nationalization and offered them a holiday from taxes.

This opening, or *infitah* as it was called in Arabic, included tourism. Sadat wanted to open Egypt's doors to hordes of wealthy travelers. There was a new openness in the political atmosphere too. Nasser was always on the lookout for enemies, but Sadat was looking for friends. Nasser had tried to govern by spying on the opposition and silencing them. Sadat preferred to win them over. "I am proud that for the first time in 40 years we have no concentration camps,"[15] he said. Sadat emptied the jails, released imprisoned journalists, and encouraged some freedom of the press. Nasser had controlled the courts; Sadat restored their independence. Each month saw new gains for democracy.

As a symbol of the new order, Sadat took a pickax and swung the first blow at the wall of an old prison that was being torn down. The damp brick crumbled and hordes of cockroaches ran out. Sadat felt he was destroying the filthy wall of cell 54.

"Many changes have come to Egypt under Sadat," said an Egyptian woman, "but Jihan is the greatest change of all."[16] Jihan was working for greater rights for women. Through her efforts the Egyptian Parliament enacted a new Civil Rights Law and she founded the Arab African Women's League. "I decided I must do something to help . . . women win respect and security, so they wouldn't be tyrannized by their husbands,"[17] she said. Jihan became the symbol of the new liberated woman in Egypt.

Not everyone approved of *infitah*. The Muslim Brotherhood and other fundamentalists opposed it. They feared that Westerners would bring their alien and permissive life-style to Egypt. They wanted to shut the door on the West, not open it further.

Most Egyptians welcomed the new openness. Foreigners were cautious. As one said, "We may sign letters of intent, but not checks, not yet."[18] They wanted a secure peace before investing their money, but the second series of peace talks between Egypt and Israel was stalled. Each side felt it was giving up everything and getting nothing in return. Kissinger abandoned his shuttle diplomacy and waited. He knew the cost of maintaining their armies was crippling both countries. Without peace, Sadat's effort to save Egypt's economy through *infitah* was doomed.

By summer, both countries wanted to get back on the shuttle diplomacy track. When Sadat opened the canal on June 5, 1975, Israel took that as a sign of good will. Israel matched it by pulling half its tanks twenty more miles to the east. Kissinger took up the stalled negotiations and on September 4, 1975, Israel and Egypt signed a second disengagement agreement. Under its terms, Israel moved still farther east, giving up the strategic Sinai mountain passes and the Sinai oil fields. Egypt agreed not to blockade Israel's access to the Red Sea. Both sides pledged not to use force against the other. But the fear and anger that existed between the two countries had not been overcome. At the signing ceremony for the second disengagement agreement, the Egyptians refused to shake the Israelis' hands or even acknowledge their presence. It wasn't war, but it wasn't peace either.

Sadat and Menachem Begin, prime minister of Israel, talk at dinner in Jerusalem (1977).

Chapter 8

JERUSALEM

"Do you know that there are two big powers in the world now that have standing armies of 700,000? The United States and the Soviet Union. And Anwar Sadat also has 700,000! Can you imagine?"[1] Sadat asked. More difficult to imagine was where he would find the money to pay for this army.

When it came to budgeting money Sadat, like other leaders, used a shorthand expression: guns or butter. By butter, Sadat meant spending money on food, housing, schools, hospitals—all the things Egyptians needed for a better life. Sadat claimed that hostilities had cost Cairo $24 billion since 1967. "Think what a paradise Egypt would be if that had been invested to develop this country,"[2] he said. Now with the war over and the second troop disengagement agreement signed, Sadat hoped to come a little closer to making that paradise a reality.

In his October Working Paper, Sadat had included programs for education and health care. Four thousand Egyptian villages were to get electricity for the first time. Sadat even talked about a new map for Egypt. "Not a single new city has been established in Egypt since the opening of the

Suez Canal . . . more than one hundred years ago."[3] He planned to establish these cities in the Western Desert, the barren land near the Libyan border. "I am all for a drive to the west," he told an American. "You know how much I like your western movies. We need the same in Egypt."[4]

Egyptians wanted this better life immediately. One thousand peasants a day poured into Cairo looking for jobs. The population exploded from two to eight million. Many lived in one room using the public faucet for water and the street for a toilet. They met others who had grown up without ever having had a bath. Cairo began falling apart. Sewage pipes burst and buildings collapsed. Buses, with passengers clinging to the roof and sides, broke down under the strain.

Gradually the optimism following the October War disappeared. *Infitah* was not providing the better life. Instead, workers found prices kept rising and there were always more mouths to feed. Sadat said, "Now, we have the highest birth rate in the world. . . . Every year, we grow by one million more people, on the narrow strip of land where we all live."[5] By 1976, Sadat predicted it would take five more years to improve Egypt's economy.

Egypt had to pay a huge foreign debt immediately. The United States advised Sadat to "bite the bullet" and cut expenses. One large government expense was the food subsidies paid to keep food prices low. Without these subsidies many Egyptians could not afford bread, let alone butter.

On January 18, 1977, Egyptians awoke to headlines proclaiming food price increases. Trouble started immediately. Factory workers marched toward Alexandria carrying petitions and shouting, "O Hero of the Crossing, where is our breakfast?"[6] Grim-faced police barred their way. Hundreds, with misery and hunger showing on their faces, poured from the slums. The police used clubs and fired warning shots. A few of the shots proved fatal. The mob retaliated with stones and bricks chanting, "You live in style and we live seven to a room. You change your clothes three times a day and we change once a year."[7]

In Cairo, marchers headed for Abdin Palace. Police could not hold them back as they ransacked restaurants and shops filled with delicacies they could never afford. Sadat was in Aswan. There were rumors that he disguised himself as a *fellah* and rode in an old taxi to the airport hoping to avoid the fury of the crowds.

Sadat was gravely disturbed by these riots. No matter how serious Egypt's financial problems, he could not solve them by cutting the food subsidies. They were quickly restored.

Meanwhile his army chiefs came with long faces warning Sadat that Egypt's weapons were out of date and inferior to Israel's. They complained because Russia refused to sell them any new equipment or even supply spare parts since Egypt still owed money on the old armaments. They explained that a disengagement of troops was not the same thing as a peace treaty and they demanded better weapons to keep up with Israel. Sadat realized that trying to pay for guns and butter was destroying Egypt. Once more he needed a radical solution.

There was a new president in the White House named Jimmy Carter. Sadat traveled to Washington to meet him. He was impressed with Carter's religious faith. They had similar backgrounds too. Both had been farmers and had grown up on the land.

Israel also had a new leader, Menachem Begin. He continued his country's search for a way to bring peace to its borders. Prime Minister Begin did something startling to prove his sincere desire for peace. Israeli agents had discovered that Colonel Qaddafi of Libya was planning to have Sadat assassinated. Begin sent this information to one of President Sadat's closest friends. Why, Sadat wondered, had his enemy's prime minister wanted to save his life? He added this piece to the Middle East puzzle.

President Carter wrote to President Sadat. But this was not the usual official letter sent from president to president. This letter was handwritten, hand-sealed, and hand-delivered. Only Carter and Sadat knew the contents. Sadat never made the letter public, although he said it recounted the history of the Middle East conflict. He never suggested the letter contained any startling or mysterious information. It wasn't the content, but its effect on Sadat that proved so important.

As Sadat reviewed the endless rounds of negotiations—the haggling and bickering he so detested—a new appraisal of the Middle East took shape. Sadat wrote back to President Carter promising a bold action. But he had no idea yet what that bold action might be.

"I began a deep and completely fresh appraisal of the situation. I realized that we were about to be caught up in a terrible vicious circle precisely like the one we'd lived through over the last thirty years. *And the root cause was... that... psychological barrier...* that huge wall of suspicion, fear, hate, and misunderstanding that has for so long existed between Israel and the Arabs. It made each side simply unwilling to believe the other.

"It was then that I drew ... on the inner strength I had developed in Cell 54 ... [a] capacity for change. ... My contemplation of life and human nature in that secluded place had taught me that he who cannot change the very fabric of his thought will never be able to change reality, and will never, therefore, make any progress."[8]

Sadat looked at the Arab-Israeli conflict in a fresh light. The fear and hatred that prevented Arabs and Israelis from trusting each other had to be changed. But how? What could one man do?

Sadat believed Begin truly wanted peace. Now he had to

convince Begin of Egypt's sincerity. The best place to do that was in Jerusalem itself, at Israel's Knesset (parliament). The picture grew clearer. In his mind's eye he imagined himself performing prayers in Jerusalem at the al-Aqsa mosque so holy to Muslims.

At first Sadat thought of inviting the big five superpowers and other Arab states to join him. Then he decided that time was too short. He would make the journey alone. "Happiness overwhelmed me . . . the happiness of a man when he gets hold of the truth after a long and painful search."[9] His foreign minister thought it was a disastrous idea and tried repeatedly to dissuade him. When every argument failed, the minister resigned.

Those attending the Egyptian People's Assembly on November 9, 1977, heard Sadat announce that he would go "to the ends of the earth if this will prevent one soldier . . . from being wounded." They sat in stunned silence when he added that he would go "to the Knesset itself"[10] in Jerusalem. Immediately after the speech, questions flew. Did he really mean it? Was it a slip of the tongue? Begin and Carter were equally confused. Neither was certain how to respond. The following day, Begin declared if President Sadat came to Jerusalem, he would be received with "all the hospitality which both the Egyptian and Israeli peoples have inherited from our common father, Abraham."

Jihan learned about the Jerusalem trip from her daughter

who announced, "Daddy is going to Jerusalem!" When Sadat came home, Jihan told him, "It's the best way to peace."[11] Sadat agreed, but knowing the tremendous risk involved, took time to write his epitaph—the inscription he wanted on his grave.

Reporters tracked Sadat constantly, wanting to know if he were really going. Sadat said he hadn't received a proper invitation. Begin immediately drafted a formal letter and asked the American ambassador to deliver it. The president of Egypt accepted. History was being made.

Meanwhile the Israeli army band made a frenzied search for the music of the Egyptian national anthem. Seamstresses worked overtime stitching Egyptian flags, and hospitals gathered quantities of blood that matched Sadat's. Israel was in a turmoil preparing not only for Sadat, but the thousands of reporters who would cover his arrival.

As the Sabbath ended at 8:00 P.M. on November 19, 1977, Sadat made the crossing and landed at Ben Gurion airport near Tel Aviv. Some people wondered how so much of the world's energy and emotion could be concentrated on the door of the plane without blowing it apart. Trumpets sounded a welcoming fanfare, followed by the deep reverberating boom of a twenty-one gun salute. Spotlights and flashlights lit the sky as Anwar el-Sadat, president of Egypt, stepped onto Israeli soil. Enemies shook hands. Then Sadat, Begin, and other dignitaries stood together solemnly listening to the Egyptian and Israeli national anthems. Throughout the audience and around the world, tears flowed freely as each person watching the event pondered its meaning. In 1973 Sadat had called Golda Meir, then Israel's prime minister, the "hated old lady." Now he said in greeting her, "Madame, I have waited a long time to meet you."[12] Later she gave Sadat gold earrings for his newest granddaughter.

Early Sunday there was trouble at al-Aqsa mosque. Sadat wanted television news coverage when he offered prayers. Palestinian Arabs opposed to his visit did not. They put pressure on the sheikh in charge of the mosque to prevent the broadcast. He banned the television unit from the front of the mosque. The Israeli army saved the day with a four-hundred-yard cord. Sadat got his broadcast from television equipment set up outside the mosque wall.

Finally, under the watchful eye of fifteen hundred security men, Sadat prayed at al-Aqsa mosque, across from the Dome of the Rock upon which Muslims believe the prophet Muhammad ascended to heaven. Then Sadat visited the Church of the Holy Sepulchre, where Christians believe Jesus was buried. Next he went to Yad Vashem, the memorial to the six million Jews who died in the Nazi holocaust.

Still to come was Sadat's speech to the Knesset. Before entering the parliament building, he placed a wreath at the memorial to Israel's war dead. Sadat spoke in Arabic saying, "There are moments in the lives of nations . . . [when]

those known for their wisdom and clarity of vision [must] survey the problem with all its complexities . . . in a bold drive toward new horizons."[13] He was speaking to Arab and Jewish leaders, asking them to throw away their prejudices and old patterns of thinking and examine the problem as if for the first time.

"How can we achieve a durable peace based on justice?" Sadat asked. "The answer is not difficult. . . . You want to live with us, in this part of the world. In all sincerity I tell you we welcome you among us with full security and safety. This in itself is a tremendous turning point, one of the landmarks of a decisive historical change. We used to reject you. We had our reasons and our fears, yes. Yet today . . . I declare it to the whole world, that we accept to live with you in permanent peace based on justice. . . . Today, through my visit to you, I ask why don't we stretch out our hands with faith and sincerity, so that together we might remove all suspicion of fear, betrayal and bad intentions . . . to erect a huge edifice of peace?"[14]

Sadat listed his terms for peace. He had not given up any of his demands for territory or for a Palestinian state. Nor did Begin give up any Israeli claims during his speech. Nothing and yet everything had changed. Four years after 222 Egyptian planes had made the crossing on a mission of destruction, one Egyptian plane made the crossing on a mission of peace.

Many considered this crossing more daring than the October War. Sadat was breaking with his Arab brothers. He was risking their fury to talk to the enemy. Risk takers know there are no guarantees. But Sadat believed his "sacred mission" had achieved its goal. "I was astounded, really by the Israeli people—children, women, everyone hailing, really hailing me. I am really startled till this moment that the barrier of distrust, bitterness, hatred and so on that has been between us during the last 30 years has been broken down in 35 hours. Amazing! Really!"[15]

Israelis who had lived with the sword of war dangling over their heads for thirty years saw, for the first time, a chance for peace if they returned the occupied territories. Now Sadat had supporters on both sides of the Sinai campaigning for its return.

Israeli leaders knew they had to make drastic decisions. If they failed Sadat, no other Arab leader would give them a second chance. Sadat was gambling everything on peace and forcing the Israelis to do so as well.

Western countries hailed Sadat as a courageous statesman. *Time* magazine voted him Man of the Year. Some Middle Eastern countries responded differently. Syria declared a national day of mourning; Iraq radio called the trip a "Pan-Arab catastrophe" and Sadat a traitor; Libyans burned the Egyptian embassy to the ground and broke diplomatic relations; and a Palestinian group swore to assassinate

Sadat for committing "the ugliest treason"[16] in Arab history.

Egyptians joyfully welcomed their president home. "When I returned home, I was astounded. . . . Something has happened to my people here," Sadat said. "It has never been like that since the start of our revolution. Even in the peak of victories, even when we nationalized the Suez Canal, it was never like this."[17]

Anwar Sadat, President Jimmy Carter, and Prime Minister Menachem Begin shake hands following the signing of the Middle East peace treaty after the Camp David meetings (1979).

Chapter 9

CAMP DAVID

"We are in an era of wonders," said Sadat. "While I was in Jerusalem, I was asked, are you going to invite Begin to Egypt? . . . I told him, how am I going to receive you in Egypt while your soldiers are still in Sinai? I couldn't convince my people. . . . When I returned to Cairo and saw the reaction of my people, it was astounding. Lots of facts which were valid a few days before, they are not valid now. . . . Yes, I shall be receiving him. . . . the act itself—its boldness—has changed everything. Everything!"[1]

Sadat made it sound simple, but everything had not changed, including the Arab and Israeli terms for peace. Any settlement was complicated by the fact that Sadat wore two hats. He spoke as president of Egypt and also as leader of the Arabs, including the Palestinians. Sometimes their interests conflicted. Then President Sadat had to make a difficult choice. Which came first? Egypt or the Arabs?

"Why did I always think we could achieve so much through peace?" asked Sadat. "By a simple calculation: how much war had cost. . . . We managed to reopen the Suez Canal. Against this we have to set the cost to Egypt of 14 billion pounds, plus all the losses in men and equipment."[2]

Egypt needed peace so Sadat could cut down military expenses. How could he make the tremendous risk of his Jerusalem trip pay off in peace? First he had to prove that Israelis could trust him. He halted anti-Israel propaganda. The program on Radio Cairo's military wavelength changed from "The Sounds of the Battlefront" to "The Flags of Peace." The government stopped printing anti-Zionist pamphlets and encouraged schools to drop negative stories about Jews and Israel.

Each step Sadat took toward Israel widened the gap between him and the Arabs. When he followed up his Jerusalem visit by calling for a meeting in Cairo, the Arab states replied: Not Coming. Instead, they met in Libya to denounce him. The Russians also criticized his Jerusalem trip and his new friendship with the United States. Sadat responded by closing Soviet cultural centers in Egypt. He had already cancelled the Treaty of Friendship with Russia.

Sadat held the Cairo conference anyway, but it was a great disappointment to him. Israel and Egypt went back to haggling over details. They spent an entire day arguing about the place cards on the round conference table. Although the Palestine Liberation Organization (PLO) was not attending the conference, the Egyptians wanted its place card on the table. The Israelis insisted it be removed. Finally they compromised by eliminating all place cards. The flags in front of the hotel had to be taken down for the same reason. Sadat could not tolerate this quibbling. He wanted decisions. In Jerusalem he had met Ezer Weizman, Israel's minister of defense. Sadat liked Weizman and invited him to Ismailia.

"What was I to say?" Weizman wondered. "How should I conduct the conversation? . . . [what] about the wars? . . . I prepared. I rehearsed."[3] He also purchased two gifts for Sadat—a pipe inscribed, "May you always smoke this pipe peacefully," and a clock inscribed, "To President Sadat, the leader who moved the clock forward."

Sadat greeted Weizman, surveyed his suit and said, "You look smart."

"I've got to be smart to meet with the greatest of Arab leaders,"[4] Weizman replied.

They both looked at the fortresses across the canal. Weizman's son had been badly wounded in one. Sadat wanted to know about the Israeli bombardment of a building bordering the path nearby. Then Sadat drew a curtain across the past. The task now was to prevent war in the future.

"I want to move quickly," he said, "we must achieve genuine peace as soon as possible."

"But there are stages,"[5] Weizman said.

"I don't want any stages," Sadat replied.

"Supposing we do reach an agreement with you," said Weizman, "what about the Syrians? . . . the Jordanians?"

"The Jordanians will follow in our footsteps. So will the

Syrians. Things in the Arab world happen the way Egypt decides."[6]

"You can't change everything so quickly, after so many years," Weizman tried to explain.

"I have changed things quickly!"[7] Sadat retorted. He did not understand why Begin hesitated to rely on these changes. Nor did Sadat have any patience with Israel's democratic system and Begin's responsibility to the Knesset.

When Begin came to Egypt there were no Israeli flags flying and Sadat did not meet Begin at the airport. Three weeks later an Egyptian delegation came to Jerusalem for more talks. Neither side was in a mood to compromise. After the Egyptians listened to Begin's speech, they called Sadat. He ordered his delegation to return home immediately.

It was a difficult time for Sadat. Isolated from both Arabs and Israel, he realized that most leaders were not risk-takers. They proceeded cautiously, step-by-step. He, Anwar el-Sadat, practiced a politics of surprise. Bold, decisive actions dominated his presidency, from firing the Soviet advisors to declaring war. These actions had changed the course of Egypt's history. For the first time since 1948, not only peace, but democracy and prosperity were within Egypt's grasp. What could Sadat do to break the deadlock?

The president of Egypt appealed to the president of the United States to take a more active role in the peace process. Carter responded by calling a summit conference at

Camp David, his presidential resort hidden away in the Maryland mountains.

Three men's political futures and countless Egyptian, Arab, and Israeli lives rested on the success or failure of Camp David. Sadat threatened war to liberate the Sinai if the peace talks failed. The Muslim Brotherhood, opposed to a peace treaty, was linked to a plot to overthrow Sadat. In Israel, some citizens rallied in support of a treaty, while others warned Begin not to give up a single settlement in Sinai or the West Bank. President Carter hoped a dramatic foreign policy achievement would help his reelection campaign. More than anything, all three men wanted peace.

Camp David—First Day

President Carter was tense but he smiled as he greeted his guests and their staffs on September 5, 1978. Reporters were barred. Three deeply religious men, one Christian, one Muslim, and one Jew, thought about the challenges ahead as they walked toward their individual wooden cabins.

Their personalities as well as their policies separated them. President Sadat liked to wear crisp sport clothes and eat alone in his cabin. He was very disciplined about his diet, rest, and exercise—walking over two miles every morning. In discussions Sadat was self-assured and stuck to the point. He wanted to concentrate on broad issues instead of small details and preferred making decisions himself rather than relying on his staff.

Prime Minister Begin usually appeared in a coat and tie, and was careful to observe the rules of protocol. Since presidents rank higher than prime ministers, he insisted on walking to Carter's cabin, never the other way around. Begin was precise about the exact meaning of every word. He relied heavily on his staff and made it clear that all decisions had to be approved by the Israeli Knesset.

President Carter tried to bridge the differences between his guests. He dressed informally and bicycled along the paths when he found time between meetings and keeping notes. He stressed flexibility.

Camp David—Second Day

Sadat met with President Carter privately, as Begin had the night before. He set out his position and promised to be flexible except on two issues: land and sovereignty. Egypt had to get all the Sinai land back with no strings attached. He hoped to reach a final framework of peace covering the Palestinian question as well as Sinai. (Begin preferred to deal only with the Sinai.) In the afternoon meeting, Begin and Sadat presented their views. Neither showed any flexibility.

Camp David—Third Day

The three leaders met. Polite discussions did not last long as Sadat and Begin shouted at each other over Jewish settlements in the Sinai. Sadat insisted they be removed and Begin refused. President Carter received a message from

Congress that started a discussion about democracy. Begin and Sadat agreed it was the best form of government. Sadat was very proud that he was turning Egypt into a democratic state. Then the heated negotiations resumed. By nightfall Begin and Sadat were not speaking to each other.

Camp David—Fourth Day

Gloom prevailed. Carter held individual talks first with Begin, then with Sadat, trying to sort out the angry words and find areas of agreement.

Camp David—Fifth Day

Carter worked on an overall proposal covering fifty separate issues that had to be settled.

Camp David—Sixth Day

Carter decided to break the tension with an outing to Gettysburg, the Civil War battlefield. He insisted that Middle East discussions were off limits during the trip, and he made sure to sit between Sadat and Begin in the car. When they returned, Carter presented his proposal to Begin. By 9:30 P.M., the Israelis were prepared to discuss it line by line. At daybreak they found a few areas where they might reach agreement.

Camp David—Seventh Day

Carter presented the American proposals to Sadat. Israeli settlements in the Sinai were a sticking point. Carter offered a compromise. He asked whether Sadat would permit Jewish settlers to live in the Sinai if Israel gave ownership of the land back to Egypt. The answer was no. "I won't give up a single inch of my land,"[8] Sadat said. Carter continued his discussions with the Israelis during the afternoon and evening. They were very discouraged and wondered how they could keep in contact with the Egyptians if Camp David failed. Their glum attitude worried the American president.

Camp David—Eighth Day

Sadat arrived at Carter's cabin in a troubled mood. He could not sign an agreement unless it was acceptable to the Arabs, he said. Later Begin argued that he could not sign an agreement that was not acceptable to the Israelis. Carter despaired of finding any agreement acceptable to both.

Camp David—Ninth Day

Sadat and Begin each sent a representative to Carter's cottage. They worked on the document together for eleven hours. When they came to an offending word they crossed it out. They left sentences vague on purpose, and postponed difficult issues for future talks.

Camp David—Tenth Day

The problem of the Sinai settlements remained. Neither Sadat nor Begin would budge. Carter could find no solution that satisfied both sides. The talks had failed. He prepared to end them.

Camp David—Eleventh Day

All three parties had agreed to issue a joint statement about their achievements before leaving. Carter's aides were preparing the document when United States Secretary of State Cyrus Vance, his face stark white, burst into the room. "Sadat is leaving," he announced. "He and his aides are already packed. He asked me to order him a helicopter!"[9] Carter tried to collect his thoughts. Finally he walked to Sadat's cabin. The two men spoke quietly. Carter explained that this hasty departure would damage United States-Egyptian relations, as well as Sadat's reputation in the Arab world. After a long, thoughtful silence, Sadat agreed to stay.

Camp David—Twelfth Day

Carter joined Sadat for a walk. Once again he searched for a compromise. Sadat refused, in the name of Egyptian sovereignty, to permit one single Israeli settler to remain in the Sinai. Sadat was able to negotiate for Egypt knowing he had the complete control and agreement of Egypt's parliament. Later Carter talked with Begin, who shouted that for him to agree to remove the settlers was "political suicide." The Knesset had to vote on the issue. He held only a slim majority. He could lose it if they vetoed his decision. For the sake of peace, Carter persisted, let the Knesset decide. For the sake of peace, Begin agreed. A breakthrough at last!

Camp David—Thirteenth Day

The delegations started packing their suitcases. Carter had just a few hours to come up with an acceptable final document. Thoroughly exhausted, he painstakingly reworked the draft. Finally, on the thirteenth day, there was agreement.

Israel would return all the Sinai to Egypt in three stages, including three air bases, oil fields, and settlements, if the Knesset approved. Egypt would establish normal diplomatic relations with Israel after the first stage of withdrawal. Negotiations on the future of the West Bank and Gaza would be held between Egypt, Jordan, Israel, and Palestinian representatives over a five-year period. The Israeli military government would be withdrawn after an Arab, self-governing unit was established. The questions of Jerusalem and West Bank sovereignty were not settled.

Sadat paid a courtesy call at Begin's cottage, where the Israelis had gathered. Defense Minister Ezer Weizman immediately poured wine for everyone, forgetting in his excitement that Sadat was a Muslim. "I'm not a heathen like you!" Sadat rebuked him, "I drink fruit juice!"[10] Later they all flew to the White House for an official signing ceremony. In front of them were two documents: Framework of Peace in the Middle East; and Framework for the Conclusion of a Peace Treaty between Egypt and Israel. According to these agreements, both nations pledged to sign a peace treaty within three months. No one knew then that the negotiations would drag on for nearly two hundred days.

For all the differences between Sadat and Begin, the thirteen days at Camp David highlighted their similarities.

Both had exhibited tremendous courage and patriotism. Both believed so fervently in peace that they were willing to sacrifice their own political futures for it. But neither would sacrifice his country, even for peace. Knowing how much to compromise and when to stand fast took great wisdom. Yet each leader met harsh criticism at home for giving away too much and getting too little. Israelis worried they were giving up the Sinai with its strategic air bases and valuable oil fields for normal relations, which could be revoked at any time. Arabs argued that Israel had gotten recognition from the largest Arab nation without giving up the West Bank, East Jerusalem, or the Golan Heights.

Sadat received a hero's welcome in Cairo, but his support was not as widespread as it appeared. Several of his own ministers resigned in protest. Arab leaders pledged to work for the fall of Sadat's peace policies. PLO leader Yasser Arafat threatened guerrilla warfare. Arab leaders meeting in Iraq offered Sadat five billion dollars to reject Camp David. Egypt's president said his country's future was not for sale. "All the billions in the world cannot buy the will of Egypt."[11]

Begin and Sadat's courage was rewarded when they won the Nobel Peace Prize. Begin went to Norway to accept the award in person. Sadat did not. His ambassador explained that, "As long as there is no peace, it is meaningless for President Sadat to sit beside President Begin's side during the Peace Prize ceremony."[12]

The time for sitting together would come when the final peace treaty was signed. Once again, negotiators from Israel and Egypt met to hammer out details. The three-month deadline passed with no treaty in sight. When negotiations reached a standstill, Carter flew to the Middle East. He planned a last-ditch effort to save the treaty. Finally in the VIP lounge of the Cairo airport, Sadat, with a grand gesture, stopped the haggling and accepted the latest version on the spot.

The tale of three cities ended in Washington, D.C., on March 26, 1979. There, in a huge tent on the White House lawn, Sadat, Begin, and Carter signed the peace treaties.

Chapter 10

PEACE WILL BE HIS PYRAMID

"I've been able to do with my head what I've never been able to do with guns,"[1] Sadat said. Supporters of the Camp David peace treaty praised him for achieving more for Egyptians and Arabs in thirteen days of peaceful negotiations than they had accomplished in thirty years of hostility and war. Libya's Colonel Qaddafi, an opponent of the treaty, declared, "I will extend unlimited support to pull the traitor Sadat down before he drags us into new infamous adventures."[2] Others accused Sadat of destroying Arab unity, deserting the Palestinians, and signing a separate peace with Israel.

Like a father disowning his son, the Arab world broke diplomatic relations with Egypt and banished it from the Arab League, the Arab Monetary Fund, the Organization of Arab Petroleum Exporting Countries, the Arab Organization of Administrative Sciences, and the Conference of Islamic States. The Arab Civil Aviation Council barred Egypt's national airline from Arab airspace and cut off flights to Egypt.

"At the beginning I was deeply hurt by my Arab brothers,"[3] Sadat said. But he was gambling that by 1980 or 1981 he could work out the Palestinian and West Bank issues to the Arabs' satisfaction and end the split. To do that he needed to build up Israeli trust. Sadat decided to speed up normalization between the two countries.

Begin and Sadat met in Egypt. They set up a hot-line telephone link between Jerusalem and Cairo. Begin agreed to return the Sinai capital of El Arish earlier than scheduled. On May 27, 1979, Anwar el-Sadat, dressed in a white admiral's uniform trimmed in gold braid, arrived in El Arish. He had not been there since that day in 1952 when he received a message from Nasser that the revolution was starting.

Now Begin and Sadat were in El Arish for a different kind of revolution. They opened the border between the two countries and established a direct airline link. Ten days later citizens were free to travel by plane or ship between Israel and Egypt. The first Israeli cargo ship sailed through the Suez Canal. A month later Egyptians along the banks of the canal waved to three Israeli warships.

When Israel and Egypt exchanged ambassadors, Sadat said, "Today we are opening another new chapter in the history of our nation."[4] Egyptians opposed to this new chapter urged that a million Palestinian flags be flown in Egypt. Sadat, who sometimes looked down on his opponents with great scorn, said, "The dogs can bark but they can't stop the caravan from moving."[5]

Sadat announced that peace negotiations with Israel were "so far down the road to success that we don't need to really worry any more about a breakdown,"[6] This turned out to be wishful thinking. The peace treaty called for autonomy, or self-rule, for Palestinians on the West Bank. But what did self-rule mean? As one United States diplomat said, "For Begin, 'autonomy' is barely a millimeter beyond what exists now. For Sadat, it's a millimeter or so short of full sovereignty."[7]

When a journalist on the American television program *Meet the Press* asked President Sadat what kind of progress had been made in the autonomy talks, he could only answer vaguely, "In this precise moment it is premature to tell anything."[8] After Egypt and Israel ended their tenth round of talks without a solution, Sadat suspended them indefinitely on May 8, 1980.

This time Sadat could not come up with any electric shock diplomacy like his dismissal of the Russians or the October War or his Jerusalem trip to save the autonomy talks. Nor could he find any electric shock solution to Egypt's economic problems. He had hoped that the Camp David peace treaty was the key at last to unlocking Western investment. But crumbling Cairo scared off most businessmen.

One of Sadat's friends showed a Western reporter that he had the latest electronic dialing telephone and he demonstrated its complex equipment. The reporter asked to make a call. "Oh, but it does not *work*," the friend said, "no dial tone."[9] Sadat knew that the estimate to fix the telephone system was twenty billion dollars.

And that was just the telephones. That same reporter was interviewing President Sadat when the lights suddenly blinked out. President Sadat never said a word. Was he wondering where to find the money for repairs? Or where to find jobs for the university graduates? The government promised them all employment and too often solved the problem by splitting one government job into two. Was Sadat wondering how long his country could afford to pay for such inefficiency? Was he worried about the corruption? The bribery? The inflation?

Only drastic reforms could save Egypt. Sadat seemed unwilling or unable to make them. These reforms would most hurt his strongest supporters: the middle class. He did not want to anger them. There were already too many who stood against him. Nasser's followers believed Egypt's destiny rested with the Arabs. They denounced Sadat for breaking with the Arabs and allying with the West. The Muslim Brotherhood stepped up its campaign for religious reform. Brotherhood members kidnapped and murdered a government minister who resisted them. Sadat ordered the terrorists arrested and tried. Many were executed.

Sadat had told Carter he was turning Egypt into a democratic state. Yet when so much opposition to his policies appeared, he resorted to Nasser's dictatorial methods to crush it. He used phone taps, spies—all the measures that caused fear and hatred in Nasser's day. Sadat seemed to have forgotten that ten years before, when he became president, he had said fear destroyed the soul of an individual and the soul of a people. He seemed to have forgotten that he had called on Egyptians to say and do what they liked as long as they broke no laws.

Now he governed under state of emergency laws, which gave him wide powers including control over the press and the courts. Sixty Egyptian writers were investigated for writing articles "threatening the security of the home front." Sadat could veto court decisions. He vetoed one that had acquitted nineteen people. They were retried and convicted.

Over sixty dissenters, including members of Parliament who criticized Camp David, were arrested. Sadat did not consider the votes in Parliament approving Camp David large enough. He dissolved Parliament and ordered new elections, although some considered this unconstitutional. When a foreign reporter asked Sadat a critical question, Sadat answered, "In other times I would have shot you, but it is democracy I am really suffering from as much as I am suffering from the opposition."[10]

Both at home and abroad, Sadat seemed to be losing control. He grew more and more restless, traveling from one to another of his ten homes. Travel arrangements were as elaborate as Farouk's palaces, which he now used. Presidential guards as well as secretaries, advisors, and a supply of his blood followed Sadat from his old home in Cairo, to the Barrages, to Giza near the pyramids, to Mit Abul-Kum, to his rest house on the beach at Marsa Matruh, to Aswan by the dam, to Ismailia overlooking the canal, to Farouk's Ras el-Tin Palace in Alexandria, and to the newest rest house at the foot of Mount Sinai.

In Mit Abul-Kum, Sadat renewed ties with his relatives and spent more time with his three oldest daughters. On one of these visits, he learned that an Italian clothing manufacturer had named him one of the ten best-dressed men in the world. "Can you believe, Camelia, that this *fellah* from Mit Abul-Kum would ever receive such recognition?"[11] he asked.

What did the prisoner of cell 54 think about this president of Egypt? Egyptians who found it harder to afford bread resented their modern pharoah. Others resented the fact that Sadat was giving away priceless and irreplaceable antiquities from the Cairo museum as gifts to foreign dignitaries. Angrily they pointed out that these belonged to Egypt. Sadat and Egypt were not the same thing, even if he thought so. They were referring to his autobiography, *In Search of Identity*. The story, he said, was "a search for identity—my own and that of Egypt. They are one and the same thing, because since childhood I have identified myself with my country—the land and the people."[12]

The land and the people needed the president's undivided attention, but Sadat seemed unable to provide it. He spent hours watching movies, especially westerns. One summer afternoon at Marsa Matruh, Sadat was visiting with the American ambassador. "'I have to think about something very quietly,' Sadat said. He sat there puffing on his pipe, the smell of sweet tobacco flooding the room, and I didn't know whether to leave or stay,"[13] the ambassador reported. Forty-five minutes later Sadat resumed the conversation. Sadat had always spent long periods in silent thought. Everyone waited for new action or policies, but little happened. Sadat did agree to resume the talks with Israel, which he had ended seventeen months before.

At this time Camelia, now divorced, decided to continue her university studies in the United States. Her father did not want her to go. Just before she left Cairo, Sadat said, "This might be the last time you see me alive."[14]

The Muslim Brotherhood and other religious groups increased their agitation for Islamic law (*sharia*) in all aspects of government. There was talk of returning to *sharia*'s strict legal code in which, for example, a thief's hand could be chopped off. The Christian Copts objected to having *sharia* apply to them.

Sadat tried to keep a balance between Muslim and Copt demands, but in June 1981 a riot broke out in Cairo as Copts attempted to set up a church. Sadat received police reports about hidden stores of arms and ammunition among Muslim and Coptic groups. He instituted a massive crackdown on all opponents. More than sixteen hundred were arrested. The Coptic pope was placed under house arrest in a monastery. More guards were sent to universities to stop student demonstrations.

The government called for a vote and reported that 99.45 percent of the voters approved these measures. Although few believed the figures, Sadat quoted these statistics to prove that he had Egyptian support. He appeared on television to reassure the people. "[Opposition] in any way or form in the streets, in the Government, in the university, in the secondary schools, in the factory, in the public sector, in the private sector, this all has ended, it has ended."[15]

But it had not ended for Khaled el-Islambuli, aged twenty-four, who had graduated with honors from artillery school in 1978. He belonged to a Muslim fundamentalist group. By February of 1981 this group was plotting to take over power in Egypt and assassinate Sadat. When Islambuli was ordered to lead a detachment of twelve guns with their trailers in the October 6 parade he said, "Very well, I accept. Let God's will be done."[16]

Three other believers joined him. Were they ready for martyrdom? All three said yes. Islambuli arranged for them to replace the soldiers who had been assigned to the gun truck. Before the parade, he left a note for his sister explaining, "what I have done, I have done for the sake of God. . . . I do not want anything for myself."[17]

Usually Sadat loved parades, but on October 6, 1981, he told Vice-President Hosni Mubarak that he was tired. Mubarak urged him to stay home, but Sadat felt it was his duty to attend. Afterward he would go to Mit Abul-Kum to visit his brother Atif's grave.

At 10:00 A.M. Sadat took his seat of honor in the front row of the reviewing stand. Islambuli had been up since 3:00 A.M. making sure the hand grenades and live ammunition were carefully hidden in the cab of his truck. The parade started. As the truck approached the reviewing stand, Islambuli put his pistol to the driver's head and ordered him to stop. Terrified, the driver braked so suddenly that the truck skidded out of line. Islambuli leaped out and threw a grenade. His three accomplices started shooting. When the firing ended, President Sadat and seven others were dead and three of the four conspirators had been captured.

At the trial, Islambuli said, "I am proud of it because the cause of religion was at stake."[18] In answer to the question, "Why did you do it?" he gave three reasons: Sadat had betrayed *sharia*, holy Koranic law; Sadat had made peace with the Jews; Sadat had persecuted and arrested Muslim leaders. When his aunt asked if he had thought how his act would affect his father and mother, Islambuli said, "No, I thought only of God."[19]

Around the world, people thought of Anwar el-Sadat, some with admiration and others with hatred. Three American presidents, Britain's Prince Charles, the president of France, the German chancellor, and Menachem Begin of Israel attended his funeral. Out of twenty-four members of the Arab League, only three sent representatives. The Syrian radio announced, "The traitor is dead. . . . It is a victory." Other Arabs took up the chant, as they danced in the streets waving flags and firing rifles in celebration.

Cairo remained unexpectedly calm as Egyptians continued preparations for the Muslim feast of sacrifice. They seemed less devastated by the loss of Anwar el-Sadat than the West. Tributes poured in. The Japanese government called him "a great gladiator for peace." President Ronald Reagan said he was a man of peace in a time of violence. Henry Kissinger considered Sadat the greatest statesman in a hundred years and said, "Peace will be his pyramid."[20]

Thousands of years ago, thousands of men put their shoulders to the task of building Egypt's pyramids. Sadat knew it would take as many dedicated people to build a pyramid of peace. He had discovered it is easier in many ways to push a boulder of stone than to dislodge prejudice and hatred. He knew that tons of seemingly indestructible rock could be reduced to grains of sand by pushing the button activating one atom bomb. Sadat gave his life for that pyramid of peace. So far it still stands.

140

FOOTNOTES

Chapter 1

1. Anwar el-Sadat, *In Search of Identity*, (New York: Harper & Row, Publishers, Inc., 1977, 1978), 5.
2. Ibid., 6.
3. Ibid., 2.
4. Ibid., 3.
5. Ibid., 2.
6. Ibid., 3.
7. Ibid.
8. Ibid., 4.
9. Ibid., 8.
10. Ibid., 11.
11. Ibid., 12.
12. Ibid., 14.

Chapter 2

1. Anwar El Sadat, *Revolt on the Nile*, (New York: The John Day Company, 1957), 12.
2. Sadat, *In Search of Identity*, 27.
3. Ibid.
4. Ibid.
5. Ibid., 28.
6. Ibid., 31.
7. Edward R.F. Sheehan, "The Real Sadat and the Demythologized Nasser," *The New York Times Magazine* (July 18, 1971): 6.
8. Sadat, *In Search of Identity*, 40.
9. Ibid., 73.
10. Ibid., 75-9.
11. Ibid., 85.

Chapter 3

1. Sadat, *In Search of Identity*, 94.
2. Gloria Emerson, "Jehan Sadat," *Vogue* (January 1980): 203.
3. Sadat, *In Search of Identity*, 97.
4. Sadat, *Revolt on the Nile*, 108.
5. Ibid.
6. Ibid., 109.
7. Ibid., 125.

8. Anwar el-Sadat, *Those I Have Known*, (New York: The Continuum Publishing Company, 1984), 6.
9. "Four Crises: A Wife's View," *Time* (January 2, 1978): 33.
10. Sadat, *Revolt on the Nile*, 143-4.
11. Sadat, *In Search of Identity*, 107-8.

Chapter 4

1. Sadat, *In Search of Identity*, 119.
2. Ibid.
3. Ibid., 116.
4. "Hero in Search of a Triumph, Gamal Abdel Nasser," *Time* (April 7, 1961): 28.
5. "Nasser's Lagacy: Hope and Instability," *Time* (October 12, 1970): 23.
6. "Actor with a Will of Iron," *Time* (January 2, 1978): 27.
7. "War or Peace in Middle East?" *Newsweek* (May 30, 1955): 38.
8. "The Rise of a New Dictator," *U.S. News & World Report* (July 6, 1956): 70.
9. "Nasser, New Dictator, Rattles His Saber," *U.S. News & World Report* (August 17, 1956): 76.
10. Ibid., 77.
11. Ibid.
12. Sadat, *In Search of Identity*, 143.
13. Dr. Gerald Kurland, *The Suez Crisis, 1956*, (Charlotteville, New York: SamHar Press, 1973), 13.
14. "Why Britain Will Risk War to Keep Canal Open," *U.S. News & World Report* (August 17, 1956): 78.
15. Sadat, *In Search of Identity*, 172.
16. Sadat, *Those I Have Known*, 134.
17. Ibid., 135.
18. Ibid.
19. Ibid.
20. Ibid., 139.
21. "The Arabs In Disaster's Wake," *Time* (June 16, 1967): 32.

22. Ibid.
23. Ibid.
24. Ibid., 34.
25. "Middle East Intransigence Renewed," *Time* (December 1, 1967): 28.
26. Sadat, *In Search of Identity*, 196.
27. Sadat, *Those I Have Known*, 82.
28. Sadat, *In Search of Identity*, 198.
29. Ibid., 203.
30. *Time*, October 12, 1970, 29.

Chapter 5

1. Sadat, *In Search of Identity*, 206.
2. Ibid.
3. Ibid.
4. Ibid., 209.
5. "O Sadat, Lead Us to Liberation," *Time* (January 18, 1971): 26.
6. *The New York Times Magazine*, 33.
7. *Time*, January 2, 1978, 33.
8. "Middle East A Preemptive Purge in Cairo," *Time* (May 24, 1971): 30.
9. Sadat, *In Search of Identity*, 224.
10. "Please Call Me Anwar," *Newsweek* (October 19, 1981): 55.
11. "Sadat on the Russians: They Didn't Want to Help," *Newsweek* (August 7, 1972): 28.
12. "Middle East: A Case of Jitters," *Time* (December 6, 1971): 36.
13. Sadat, *In Search of Identity*, 230.
14. Mohamed Heikal, *The Road to Ramadan*, (New York: Quadrangle/The New York Times Book Co., 1975), 181.
15. Michael I. Handel, *The Diplomacy of Surprise: Hitler, Nixon, Sadat*, (Cambridge: Center for International Affairs, Harvard University, 1981), 277.
16. "The World Will No Longer Laugh," *Time* (October 22, 1973): 50.
17. Sadat, *In Search of Identity*, 214-5.
18. Ibid., 215.

Chapter 6

1. Sadat, *In Search of Identity*, 234-5.
2. Ibid., 240.
3. Ibid., 241.
4. "The Deadly New Weapons," *Time* (October 22, 1973): 38.
5. Sadat, *In Search of Identity*, 245.
6. Camelia Sadat, *My Father and I*, (New York: Macmillan Publishing Company, 1985), 111.
7. Sadat, *In Search of Identity*, 246.
8. Ibid., 247.
9. Ibid., 248.
10. *Time*, January 2, 1978, 33.
11. Sadat, *In Search of Identity*, 249.
12. Ibid., 244.
13. "Arabs v. Israelis in a Suez Showdown," *Time* (October 29, 1973): 22.
14. *Time*, October 22, 1973, 49.
15. Ibid.
16. Sadat, *In Search of Identity*, 253.
17. Sadat, *Those I Have Known*, 95.
18. Ibid., 47-8.
19. Ibid., 25.
20. "Sadat: Egypt Has 'Restored Its Honor,'" *Time* (October 29, 1973): 29.
21. Sadat, *In Search of Identity*, 260.
22. Ibid., 261.
23. *Time*, January 2, 1978, 33.
24. Sadat, *In Search of Identity*, 261.
25. Ibid., 262-3.
26. Ibid., 266.
27. Ibid., 267-8.

Chapter 7

1. Sadat, *In Search of Identity*, 132.
2. "The Divine Disturber of the Peace," *People* (February 25, 1980): 87.
3. Sadat, *In Search of Identity*, 269.
4. Ibid., 268.
5. "In Israel, a Sense of Foreboding," *U.S.*

News & World Report (February 11, 1974):
29.
6. Sadat, *In Search of Identity*, 268.
7. Ibid., 291.
8. Howard M. Sachar, *Egypt and Israel*,
(New York: Richard Marek Publishers,
1981), 243.
9. Ibid., 244.
10. "Anwar Sadat: Architect of a New
Mideast," *Time* (January 2, 1978): 14.
11. Sadat, *In Search of Identity*, 275.
12. "Suez Reopening: 'Ya Sadat,'" *Time*
(June 16, 1975): 26.
13. Ibid.
14. President Mohamud Anwar el Sadat,
The October Working Paper, (Ministry
of Information, Information Service,
April, 1974), 64.
15. "Plans and Dreams for Egypt," *Time*
(May 20, 1974): 46.
16. "Egypt's Liberating First Lady," *Time*
(February 18, 1974): 45.
17. Ibid.
18. "Egypt: Hungry for Peace," *U.S. News
& World Report* (January 6, 1975): 38.

Chapter 8

1. "Anatomy of a 'Bold Action,'" *Time*
(January 2, 1978): 32.
2. "A Watershed Week for Egypt's Sadat,"
Time (June 9, 1975): 28.
3. Sadat, *The October Working Paper*, 82.
4. "Sadat Opens the Door," *Time* (May 20,
1974): 45.
5. Raphael Israeli, *The Public Diary of
President Sadat*, (Leiden, the
Netherlands: E.J. Brill, 1979), 1240.
6. David Hirst and Irene Beeson, *Sadat*,
(London: Faber and Faber, 1981), 244.
7. Michael R. Burrell and Abbas R.
Kelidar, *The Washington Papers 48:
Egypt: The Dilemmas of a Nation—*

1970-1977, (Beverly Hills: Sage
Publications, 1977), 6.
8. Sadat, *In Search of Identity*, 302-3.
9. Sadat, *Those I Have Known*, 105.
10. Hirst and Beeson, *Sadat*, 255.
11. *Time*, January 2, 1978, 33.
12. "Sadat's 'Sacred Mission,'" *Time*,
(November 28, 1977): 28.
13. Lester A. Sobel, *Peace-Making in the
Middle East*, (New York: Facts on File,
Inc., 1980), 172.
14. Ibid., 173-4.
15. *Time*, January 2, 1978, 31.
16. *Time*, November 28, 1977, 39.
17. *Time*, January 2, 1978, 31.

Chapter 9

1. *Time*, January 2, 1978, 31.
2. Sadat, *Those I Have Known*, 106-7.
3. Ezer Weizman, *The Battle for Peace*,
(New York: Bantam Books, 1981), 86.
4. Ibid., 87.
5. Ibid., 88.
6. Ibid., 89.
7. Ibid., 88.
8. Ibid., 369.
9. Jimmy Carter, *Keeping Faith*, (New
York: Bantam Books, 1982), 391.
10. Weizman, *Battle for Peace*, 377.
11. Sachar, *Egypt and Israel*, 292.
12. Sobel, *Peace-Making*, 236.

Chapter 10

1. *Newsweek*, October 19, 1981, 55.
2. "Sadat: The Hour of Decision," *Time*,
(December 5, 1977): 38.
3. "In a Revealing Moment," *People*,
(November 24, 1980): 46.
4. Sobel, *Peace-Making*, 269.
5. Morton Kondracke, "The War Against
Sadat," *The New Republic* (June 2,
1979): 12.
6. Sobel, *Peace-Making*, 269.

143

7. "The Road to El Arish," *Time* (April 16, 1979): 58.
8. *Meet the Press*, September 9, 1979, 1.
9. Gail Sheehy, "The Riddle of Sadat," *Esquire* (January 30, 1979): 37.
10. "Assassination in Egypt," *New York Times* (October 7, 1981): All.
11. Sadat, *My Father and I*, 152.
12. Sadat, *In Search of Identity*, 314.
13. *Newsweek*, October 19, 1981, 55.
14. Sadat, *My Father and I*, 158.

15. *New York Times*, October 7, 1981, All.
16. Mohamed Heikal, *Autumn of Fury*, (London: Andre Deutsch, 1983), 242.
17. Ibid., 253.
18. "The Men in the Steel Cage," *Time* (December 14, 1981): 49.
19. Heikal, *Autumn of Fury*, 253.
20. Henry A. Kissinger, "A Man With a Passion for Peace," *Time* (October 19, 1981): 33.

From *The Road to Ramadan* by Mohamed Heikal. Copyright © 1975 by Times Newspapers Ltd. and Mohamed Heikal. Published by Quadrangle/The New York Times Book Co., New York.

From *The Diplomacy of Surprise: Hitler, Nixon, Sadat* by Michael I. Handel. Copyright © 1981 by the President and Fellows of Harvard College. Published by the Center for International Affairs, Harvard University, Cambridge.

Reprinted with permission of Macmillan Publishing Company from MY FATHER AND I by Camelia Sadat. Copyright © 1985 by Camelia Sadat.

Various quotes from PEOPLE magazine.

From *Egypt and Israel* by Howard M. Sacher. Copyright © 1981 by Howard M. Sacher. Published by the Putnam Publishing Group, New York.

The October Working Paper by President Mohamed Anwar el Sadat. Ministry of Information, State Information Service, 1974.

From *The Public Diary of President Sadat* by Raphael Israeli. Copyright © 1979. Published by E.J. Brill, Leiden, the Netherlands.

From *Sadat* by David Hirst and Irene Beeson. Copyright © by David Hirst and Irene Beeson. Published by Faber and Faber, London.

From *The Washington Papers 48: Egypt: The Dilemmas of a Nation—1970-1977* by Michael R. Burrell and Abbas R. Kelidar. Copyright © 1977. Published by Sage Publications, Beverly Hills.

From *Peace-Making in the Middle East*, edited by Lester A. Sobel. © 1980 by Facts On File, Inc. Reprinted by permission of Facts on File, Inc., New York.

From THE BATTLE FOR PEACE by Ezer Weizman. Copyright © 1982 by Ezer Weizman. Reprinted by permission of Bantam Books, Inc. All rights reserved.

From *Keeping Faith* by Jimmy Carter. Copyright © 1982 by Jimmy Carter. Published by Bantam Books, New York.

The New Republic, June 2, 1979.

Meet the Press, September 9, 1979.

Esquire magazine, January 30, 1979.

The New York Times, October 7, 1981.

From *Autumn of Fury* by Mohamed Heikal. Copyright © 1983 by Mohamed Heikal. Published by Random House, New York.

Anwar el-Sadat 1918-1981

1918 Anwar el-Sadat is born on December 25. Gamal Abdel Nasser (later president of Egypt) is born. American President Woodrow Wilson sets forth his Fourteen Points for World Peace. Armistice is signed between the Allies and Germany ending World War I.

1919 Treaty of Versailles is signed between Allies and Germany. Riots in Egypt.

1920 The League of Nations comes into being. The U.S. votes against joining the League. The League of Nations gives Great Britain the mandate for Palestine. Mahatma Gandhi emerges as India's leader in its struggle for independence from the British.

1921 Britain proposes abolishing its protectorate in Egypt. Adolf Hitler's storm troopers begin to terrorize political opponents. Anti-Jewish riots in Palestine.

1922 British Protectorate in Egypt ends. Britain formally recognizes the Kingdom of Egypt under Fuad I. Benito Mussolini forms Fascist government in Italy.

1923 Egypt adopts a constitution. Britain retains the right to keep troops in Egypt.

1924 Britain refuses Egypt's demand to evacuate the Sudan. Britain's governor-general of the Sudan is assassinated in Cairo. British expel Egyptian troops from the Sudan.

1925 Sadat family moves from Mit Abul-Kum to Cairo.

1928 Egyptian parliament is dissolved and freedom of the press suspended.

1929 Egyptian constitution is restored. Muslim Brotherhood is founded. Arabs attack Jews in Palestine following disputes over Jewish use of the Wailing Wall.

1930 Passfield White Paper on Palestine suggests that Jewish immigration be halted. In German elections Nazis gain over 100 seats from the center parties.

1933 Hitler is appointed German chancellor. Franklin D. Roosevelt is inaugurated as president of U.S. Japan withdraws from the League of Nations. The first concentration camps are erected by the Nazis in Germany and the boycott of Jews begins.

1934 Hitler and Mussolini meet in Venice. Hitler is elected führer. Winston Churchill warns British Parliament of the German air menace.

1935 King Fuad of Egypt dies and is succeeded by his son Farouk. Anglo-Egyptian treaty is signed ending British occupation of Egypt, except for Canal Zone, and permitting Egypt to expand its army. Sadat enters the Royal Military Academy. An Arab High Committee is formed to combat Jewish claims. Hitler and Mussolini proclaim Rome-Berlin axis.

1938 Germany annexes Austria. Sadat graduates from Royal Military Academy and is stationed at Manqabad where he meets Gamal Nasser.

1939 Germany annexes Czechoslovakia. Italy annexes Albania. Soviet-Nazi pact is signed. Germany attacks Poland. Britain and France declare war on Germany.

1940 Germany invades Denmark, Norway, Holland, Belgium, and Luxembourg. Fall of France. Battle of Britain. Germany, Italy, and Japan sign military and economic pact. Sadat marries Ekbal Madi.

1941 Japan attacks Pearl Harbor. U.S. and Britain declare war on Japan. U.S. declares war on Germany and Italy. Sadat is arrested by the British, questioned, and released. British defeat Italian forces in North Africa. Rommel begins German offensive against British in North Africa.

1942 Rommel wins battles against British in North Africa. German troops march across Egypt to El Alamein where they are defeated. Sadat is arrested and jailed for anti-British activities. The murder of millions of Jews in Nazi gas chambers begins.

1944 Sadat escapes from jail.

1945 Roosevelt dies. Germany surrenders. U.S. drops two atom bombs on Japan. Japan surrenders. The charter of the United Nations is signed. Egypt demands revision of Anglo-Egyptian treaty; end of military occupation; control of Sudan. Arab League is founded in Cairo.

1946 Sadat is arrested and jailed as conspirator in assassination of Osman. General strike in Cairo. British troops begin withdrawal from Cairo to Canal Zone. Guerrilla war in Palestine. Britain blockades ships bringing Jewish immigrants to Palestine in excess of quota.

1947 British return Palestine mandate to United Nations. U.N. proposes to partition Palestine into Arab and Jewish states. Jews accept plan; Arabs reject it. Arabs and Jews battle in Palestine.

1948 The Jewish state of Israel is proclaimed. First Arab-Israeli War begins as Egypt and other Arab armies invade Israel. Sadat is acquitted in Osman assassination case after lengthy trial.

1949 Armistice is signed in Arab-Israeli War. Sadat marries Jihan Raouf. Israel is admitted to the U.N. and moves its capital from Tel Aviv to Jerusalem.

1950 Sadat is reinstated as a captain in the Egyptian army.

1951 U.N. asks Egypt to end its 3-year-old blockade of Suez Canal to ships carrying cargo to Israel. Egypt refuses.

1952 Anti-British riots in Egypt. The Free Officers under Nasser seize power. Major General Muhammad Naguib is named premier. King Farouk abdicates. The constitution of 1923 is abolished.

1953 Egypt is declared a republic. Muslim Brotherhood is outlawed. Egypt blockades Strait of Tiran.

1954 Naguib is ousted and Nasser takes over as premier and head of state in Egypt. Anglo-Egyptian treaty is signed providing all British troops will leave Canal Zone within two years. Leaders of Muslim Brotherhood executed.

1955 Egypt purchases arms from Czechoslovakia. *Fedayeen* raids on Israel along Jordanian border and Gaza Strip increase.

1956 Nasser becomes Egypt's first elected president. New constitution is enacted. Last British troops leave Canal Zone. The U.S. and Britain inform Egypt that they will not finance the Aswan Dam. Nasser nationalizes the Suez Canal. Egypt, Jordan, and Syria unite their military forces. The second Arab-Israeli War begins (Suez War). Israel invades Sinai; British and French land troops and bomb Egypt's airfields but are forced to withdraw under pressure from U.S. and U.S.S.R.

1957 Israeli forces withdraw from Sinai. U.N. observers are stationed along the Egyptian frontier. Israeli ships are permitted through Tiran Strait. U.N. reopens Suez Canal. Nasser nationalizes foreign banks and businesses.

1958 Egypt and Syria unite forming United Arab Republic (U.A.R.) with Nasser as president. Yemen agrees to federate with U.A.R. U.S.S.R. grants loan to U.A.R. to build Aswan Dam.

1960 Sadat has heart attack. John F. Kennedy is elected president of U.S.

1961 Syria secedes from U.A.R. Egypt is only country in U.A.R. after Nasser dissolves Egypt's union with Yemen and sends troops to Yemen to support republican forces.

1963 Kennedy is assassinated and Lyndon B. Johnson becomes president.

1967 Egypt (U.A.R.) requests that U.N. Emergency Force leave Sinai and Gaza ending its 10-year peace-keeping role in Middle East. Egypt doubles its troops in Sinai and closes Strait of Tiran to Israeli ships. Jordan and Egypt sign mutual defense pact. Third Arab-Israeli War begins (Six-Day War) as fighting breaks out in Sinai and Jerusalem. Israel destroys Egyptian, Syrian, and Jordanian air forces in surprise attacks and conquers East Jerusalem, Sinai, Gaza Strip, and East Bank of Jordan River. Egypt closes Suez Canal. Nasser offers to resign but stays in office by popular demand. U.N. Security Council adopts Resolution 242 requiring: Israel withdraw from all conquered territory; each country recognize territory of other states; free navigation through international waterways.

1968 Nasser begins "War of Attrition" against Israel. Riots in Egypt lead to closing of universities. Richard M. Nixon is elected president of U.S.

1969 Nasser appoints Sadat vice-president. Golda Meir becomes Israel's prime minister. Fighting along Suez Canal. Syria attacks Israeli post. Egypt repudiates U.N. cease-fire and calls for all-out war with Israel. U.S. Secretary of State William Rogers proposes Middle East peace plan.

1970 Aswan Dam begins operation. Israel and Egypt accept a 90-day cease-fire. Fighting in Jordan between army and Palestinian guerrillas—1500 guerrillas are captured. Nasser dies of heart attack. Sadat becomes president of Egypt.

1971 Sadat announces new peace initiative after extending cease-fire with Israel. Sadat arrests Ali Sabri and other pro-Soviet ministers as leaders of attempted coup. Sadat signs Treaty of Friendship with U.S.S.R.

1972 Sadat orders Soviet advisers out of Egypt. Arab terrorists kill Israeli Olympic athletes in Munich. Arab-Israeli violence continues in the Middle East.

1973 Fourth Arab-Israeli War begins (Yom Kippur War). Egyptian forces cross Suez Canal and Syria attacks Golan Heights. Arabs cut oil production causing world oil crisis. After heavy losses on both sides, an unstable cease-fire is established. First Arab-Israeli peace conference in Geneva.

1974 Henry Kissinger's "shuttle diplomacy" results in a disengagement agreement between Egypt and Israel. U.S. and Egypt renew diplomatic relations. Syria and Israel agree on disengagement.

1975 Sadat leads convoy that reopens Suez Canal. Egyptians and Israelis sign second disengagement agreement.

1976 Egypt cancels Treaty of Friendship with Soviets.

1977 Jimmy Carter becomes president of U.S. Menachem Begin becomes prime minister of Israel. Egyptian workers demonstrate against price rises. Sadat goes to Jerusalem. Begin visits Egypt. *Time* magazine names Sadat Man of the Year.

1978 Sadat, Begin, and Carter hold peace talks at Camp David. They sign two documents: A Framework for Peace in the Middle East and A Framework for the Conclusion of a Peace Treaty between Israel and Egypt. Sadat and Begin win the Nobel Peace Prize.

1979 Sadat and Begin meet in Washington, D.C. to sign a peace treaty ending the state of war between the two countries. Eighteen Arab League countries and the PLO sever diplomatic relations with Egypt and impose an economic boycott. Egypt and Israel open their borders and establish air link.

1980 Further Middle East talks flounder on issue of Palestinian autonomy. Sadat visits Washington to discuss Israeli settlements with Carter.

1981 Sadat adopts repressive measures. Riots erupt between Muslim extremists and Coptic Christians. Sadat orders mass arrests. Sadat is assassinated while watching a victory parade on October 6.

INDEX- *Page numbers in boldface type indicate illustrations.*

ABOUT THE AUTHOR

Deborah Nodler Rosen has pursued a lifelong interest in history. Along the way she graduated with honors from Wellesley College where she majored in history and earned a J.D. from the University of Pennsylvania. In 1960 she was the recipient of a Fullbright Fellowship. Her writing includes two American history textbooks and numerous travel and feature articles. In her travels she has visited Egypt and the Middle East and presently lives in Winnetka, Illinois with her husband and two children.

B
SADAT

Rosen, Deborah
Nodler.

Anwar el-Sadat.

**MADISON JUNIOR HIGH SCHOOL
DIXON ILLINOIS**